Land of
Enchantment

LEIGH STEIN

Land of
Enchantment

❧ ❧ ❧

A PLUME BOOK

PLUME
An imprint of Penguin Random House LLC
375 Hudson Street
New York, New York 10014

Library of Congress Cataloging-in-Publication Data

Names: Stein, Leigh, 1984– author.
Title: Land of Enchantment / Leigh Stein.
Description: New York, New York : Plume, 2016. | Includes bibliographical references.
Identifiers: LCCN 2015046893| ISBN 9781101982679 (hardcover) |
ISBN 9781101982686 (ebook)
Subjects: LCSH: Stein, Leigh, 1984—Relations with men. | Stein, Leigh, 1984—Homes and haunts—New Mexico. | Coming of age—New Mexico. | Young women—New Mexico—Biography. | Couples—New Mexico—Biography. | Man-woman relationships—New Mexico. | Abusive men—New Mexico—Biography. | Abusive men—United States—Death. | Grief—United States. | Women authors, American—21st century—Biography. | BISAC: BIOGRAPHY & AUTOBIOGRAPHY / Personal Memoirs. | FAMILY & RELATIONSHIPS / General. | FAMILY & RELATIONSHIPS / Death, Grief, Bereavement.
Classification: LCC PS3619.T465 Z46 2016 | DDC 813/.6 [B]—dc23
LC record available at https://lccn.loc.gov/2015046893

Printed in the United States of America
10 9 8 7 6 5 4 3 2 1

Page v: Lines from "It was trigger-happy" from *Bandit Letters* by Sarah Messer. Copyright © 2008. Reprinted by permission of New Issues Poetry and Prose.

Pages 65 and 67: Two excerpts [6l.] from "Elm" from *Ariel* by Sylvia Plath. Copyright © 1963 by Ted Hughes. Reprinted by permission of HarperCollins Publishers.

Book design by Eve L. Kirch

Penguin is committed to publishing works of quality and integrity.
In that spirit, we are proud to offer this book to our readers;
however, the story, the experiences, and the words
are the author's alone.

It was outlands, no trespassing, possession without address, want, cheating, double-crossing horse-thievery, here why not take all my chips, you still owe me money, asshole, out past the barbed wire. The roads with no road signs, out in a place where people can slap each other, smash cooked eggs, a skillet against the kitchen wall of a shack in the desert where the cactus throw their limbs in the air like dance hall melodrama, and I have escaped to tell you all of this.

Sarah Messer, "It was trigger-happy"

What Jessica valued, perhaps more than the relationship, was the evidence of it.

Adrian Nicole LeBlanc, *Random Family*

Land of
Enchantment

A Hot Night in Late July
(2011)

I was with him the day he got the motorcycle, a 1988 Honda Nighthawk—1988 for the year he was born. We had matching leather jackets for when we rode through the desert, two silhouettes against the night. In a box somewhere I still had my helmet, a souvenir from the woman I was when we were together.

It was a hot night in late July when I got the news. My new boyfriend had central AC at his apartment, so that's where we were, sitting on the couch with our bare feet propped on an ottoman that doubled as a coffee table. Chinese takeout. Channel surfing. I'd stopped the remote on *My Big Fat Gypsy Wedding*, a reality show about poor young Traveler women getting married like queens.

The first time the phone rang, the caller ID said it was Jason, so I didn't pick up. I'd been avoiding his calls for the past six weeks, ever since he visited me in Brooklyn and we got in a fight at the Coney Island Mermaid Parade; we got in a fight in Central Park in the rain; we got high and we got drunk and we killed time until he finally flew back to Little Rock and I decided it was *really over* this time.

For the past couple of days, Jason had been calling more frequently, so when my phone rang a second time, I wasn't surprised, but this time, it was an unknown number. I let the call go to voice mail. On TV, a housewife was demonstrating how she cleaned her teeth with Clorox, straight from the bottle. I was watching her and my boyfriend Brian was watching me, as I listened to the message. The caller identified himself as Jason's half brother in Birmingham. I recognized the accent they shared, but we'd never met, or even spoken before.

"What did he say?" Brian asked.

"He just asked me to call him back."

"Maybe he's calling to tell you Jason killed himself," he said, and my stomach dropped—not because I thought he might be right, but because Brian had come up with an explanation for the evening's phone calls before I'd even begun to wonder if something was wrong.

I called the number in Birmingham back.

His brother's voice was calm and unemotional. There was a motorcycle accident. Jason had not "made it." For one sweet second, I thought it was a joke. A cruel one, sure, but Jason had never been above cruelty, and it wasn't hard to imagine him coming up with this scenario in order to punish me for refusing his calls. I held my breath and waited to hear his laughter in the background, for him to come on the line and say, *Gotchou.* Meanwhile, I watched a muted trailer-park bride corset herself into a gown studded with roses made from Swarovski crystal and climb into a black limousine. Why didn't I turn off the TV? It was a Saturday night in late July. Jason had been dead since Thursday.

When it was clear that no one was waiting in the background, I apologized to his brother for thinking he was Jason and not answering his calls sooner. "I decided to stop talking to him . . . recently," I tried to explain.

"I figured as much," he said, not unkindly.

I promised to look into plane tickets to Little Rock, even though a part of me wondered whether I should even go to the funeral. Already I could feel the pins and needles of old insecurities, and didn't want to be there, just one ex-girlfriend among many, queuing up for my turn to say why I thought what we had was so special. *I was with him the day he got the motorcycle*, I could say. *We had matching leather jackets.*

After we said good-bye, I borrowed Brian's laptop to Google Jason's name, because if something had really happened, if this wasn't a joke, then proof of it would be online. There wasn't an obituary yet, but I found a memorial page where people were leaving condolences and animated gifs of flickering candles that would never expire. I had the option to "sign the memory book" or "light a candle," but I couldn't even begin to think of any condolences to offer, when I just wanted to be consoled myself. Brian was beside me, but he might as well have been a stranger I'd picked up at a bar. We hadn't known each other long enough for him to have heard all the stories of who I was before I met him.

The only other result I could find on Google was an article in an Arkansas newspaper about Jason: "Man accused of stabbing another in brawl." Eleven days before the accident, Jason had been arrested for stabbing a man in the stomach outside a gas station. When the police officer asked about all the blood on the concrete, Jason admitted "someone might have gotten cut," and pulled a knife from his pocket.

In the comments section at the bottom of the article, someone had written "SAD DUMB THUGS."

"Jason stabbed someone," I told Brian, "before he died."

"Why?"

"I don't know." I shook my head, trying to clear it. This was the kind of violent act that I always knew he was capable of, and that I used to worry I would be the victim of. I didn't know what kind of woman that made me, if I still loved and missed a man like that. If I still wanted him to come back.

The Pin-Pen Switch

(2007)

Jason and I met at an audition for a tragedy. It was late February, and all of Chicago was blanketed in snow. I'd come prepared with a monologue, but the assistant director asked if I wouldn't mind also reading a scene—there was one guy left who didn't have a partner.

Approaching me, Jason smiled, and then looked at the floor. He was tall and athletic, wearing jeans and a gray T-shirt that read *BRUCE LEE IS MY HOMEBOY* over a thermal undershirt. He looked like the popular jock from every teen movie; I could imagine a slow-motion shot of him walking along a wall of lockers with his arm around a girl. Under any other circumstances, I wouldn't have even known how to start a conversation with him. He would have been the one to come up to me, to ask if he could borrow my geometry homework.

I introduced myself and said I was auditioning for Medea, who was he auditioning for?

He said his name was Jason, but he didn't know what the play was about; he just auditioned for whatever the drama department offered.

"Jason is Medea's husband's name," I said. "Like Jason and the Argonauts?" He stared at me. I babbled on: "Basically, he leaves his wife for this rich princess, and so Medea gets revenge by murdering their children and riding off in a chariot."

"How old are you?" he said.

"Twenty-two. How old are you?"

"How old do you think I am?"

I guessed twenty-one, but he wouldn't say if I was right or wrong.

We found an empty stairwell where we could run lines, but it was hard to get started. Up close, Jason's skin glowed soft and golden. His eyes were sea-glass green. He had a slightly upturned Irish nose and a default sneer that bloomed into a bright, disarming smile when I said or did something amusing. Each time the sides of our arms or legs brushed against each other, I felt a pinch of pleasure, the sting of wanting more. I made myself stare at the script in my lap.

"So why do you know so much about this play?" he asked.

"When I was nineteen, I moved to New York to go to acting school," I continued. "I love Greek tragedy. My monologue is from *Alcestis*," I said, eager to impress him with where I'd been and what I'd done in order to distract him from what I looked like.

With my round, moony face, protruding elfish ears, and plain dark hair I never styled, there wasn't a chance I was in his league. My expressive eyes were my only good feature, and I'd lined them in black for the audition. Self-conscious about weighing twenty pounds more than I had in high school, I hadn't taken off my clothes for anyone in a year—not since I'd dated my thirty-six-year-old manager, who told me I wasn't allowed to mention our relationship to anyone at the restaurant where we worked, and then stopped returning my phone calls after I told him I was a virgin. For a year I'd been kicking myself. Why hadn't I just kept my mouth shut and let him give me what I wanted? At twenty-two, my virginity was something I had to get rid of, fast, or it would be too late for me.

The more Jason smiled at me, or laughed at things I said, the more it seemed like we were flirting with each other, but I didn't trust my own assessment of the situation. Maybe Jason was gay. It made more sense that an attractive gay man would find me funny and smart than it did for an attractive straight man to be interested in me.

Eventually we read through the script a couple of times. In the scene, Medea is confronting Jason after he has abandoned her and their children and taken a new wife.

You did well / To come, she says, *for I can speak ill of you and lighten / My heart, and you will suffer while you are listening.* Then Medea proceeds to recap their love story: first she saved his life from some fire-breathing bulls, then she slew the dragon guarding the Golden Fleece so that Jason could capture it and win the throne of Iolcus. When Pelias, king of Iolcus, went back on his word and wouldn't give it up, Medea tricked his daughters into killing their own father. To Jason, she says bitterly, *This is how I behaved to you, you wretched man, / And you forsook me, took another bride to bed.*

While we waited for our turn to see the director, I followed him outside for a cigarette break. There'd been a blizzard the night before, with forty-mile-an-hour winds and lightning that shot its way east from Iowa—the first "thundersnow" storm since 1891, the forecasters said. I was at my friend Vadim's house-warming party when it started to hail, and spent the night so I wouldn't kill myself driving home. Vadim was a sweet, tall, handsome, talented, brilliant guy. More important, he adored me. So what was my problem? Why couldn't I just fall in love with him? My parents were baffled. For whatever reason, I felt compelled to chase the difficult (an acting career) and the forbidden (the relationship with my manager). All night I stared at the ceiling in Vadim's bedroom—he took the couch—trying to recalibrate my feelings so that this night could be the beginning of our future together. It didn't work. By morning, I was so tired and grumpy from having slept wearing my contact lenses that I considered skipping the audition entirely. But here I was, standing outside in the cold, wide-awake.

Jason gestured toward the dark, snowy landscape beyond. "I did all this," he said.

"You made it snow?"

"No, I work for the school, landscaping the grounds." I noticed his work boots.

I wasn't a smoker, but I asked for a Marlboro, just to prolong the time we spent out there, away from everyone else.

"Where do you come from?" I asked. Jason didn't sound, or dress, like any of the guys I'd gone to high school, or acting school, with.

"Alabama. Arkansas. Tennessee." He inhaled. "I was All-State wrestling in Tennessee in high school. We moved around a lot for my stepdad's job. In Corpus Christi I could hold bread in my hands by the water and birds would come and get it. But my dad lives here." *Birds would come and git it.* Jason said *git* for *get* and *pin* for *pen* and *did* for *dead.* In dialect studies, this is called the pin-pen switch. *Gold star, Leigh*, I thought to myself. *What are you going to do with that information?*

"I don't usually get along with people," I blurted out, trying to put into words what I sensed we might have in common. The truth was I got along with everybody, but there was a disconnect between my outgoing Midwestern cheerfulness and the nagging feeling that I was different, strange, destined to live somewhere other than the place I had come from.

"Me either," Jason said. "What are you doing later?"

I have almost completely forgotten our actual audition in front of the director, but I remember every beat of our time in the cold, the color and texture of his coat when I stood close, what his face looked like when he was blowing smoke.

When the audition was over, I called my mom and told her I had met someone and would be home late.

"That's great, Leigh," she said. I was living at home in the suburbs with my parents again, for the third time as an adult, after buckling under the stress of trying to piece together a living in New York (twice), and then losing my sublet in Chicago. Some of my friends in New York had parents who paid their expenses while they "figured things out." I had parents who let me move back into my childhood bedroom while I did the same. When Jason told me he lived alone, I was impressed.

First we drove to the supermarket to get some groceries.

"You make me really nervous," Jason said in the pasta aisle. *I* made *him* nervous? "Wait, why?"

9

"Because you're pretty and nice *and* smart. Can I hold your hand?"

I gave it to him. Mine was cold and his was warm. The middle-aged checkout ladies smiled at us; they all knew his name. I felt like I'd been cast in some role I'd never even dreamed of playing.

We drove back to his apartment and had a snowball fight in the soft yellow light of the parking lot, laughing and pushing each other into snowbanks. Once inside, I borrowed a pair of clean socks because the snow had soaked through my boots, and he cleared the bedding from the couch. He told me that's where he slept every night, instead of the bed, because it was less lonely in there with the TV on.

"Do you like Kool-Aid?"

I had to think about it. "I'm not sure if I've had it since I was eight," I said.

For dinner, he cooked penne Alfredo with Ragú sauce from a jar, and stirred a pitcher of blue Kool-Aid. Then we made out on the couch for a while. The Oscars played in the background; we pretended we were watching.

Every time I moved back in with my parents, I had an escape plan, and this time was no different: I was working on my application to a directing program at a theater school in Montreal. *This will be perfect*, I thought. *We can have snowball fights and fool around until I move to Canada.*

"Do you have a Facebook?" he asked.

"Yeah," I said. "Do you?"

"Friend me."

By the time I got home that night, he had removed his date of birth from his profile, so I wouldn't know he was only eighteen years old. I turned off my phone and went to sleep. When I woke up the next day, there was a voice mail from him, left in the early hours of the morning.

"Leigh," the message said. "I don't actually hate spending time with you. We should go out sometime. Okay, 'bye."

When I called back he said he'd stayed up late Googling me and reading my poems. "They're very . . . Jewish."

"'Jewish'?"

"Jewish," he repeated.

"Oh, I know which one you read. . . ." The poem that begins, *Miriam danced in Exodus while the Red Sea drowned the horses. . . .*

"Can you look at my English paper that's due in an hour and twelve minutes?"

Was he serious? "I have to go to work," I said.

"I'll e-mail you the outline now and you can look at the real paper later. What are you doing this weekend? Want to go out?"

"Sure," I said.

"I just asked you out," he said.

"And I said, 'Sure.'"

After we hung up, I wrote in my diary, *There must be something horribly wrong with him I haven't discovered yet.*

Torch Song

(2007)

I grew up in the dark—in basements, in bedrooms, backstage in the wings behind the velvet. I grew up at sleepovers where the girls with the power were the ones who came up with the most humiliating dares for the others. We didn't realize the name for what we all wanted so badly was *power*; the closest we could get was *attention*, standing outside in the middle of the night unsupervised, lifting our shirts to flash our small breasts to streetlights, screaming the words we weren't allowed to say in daylight. *When were our real lives finally going to start? When and how would we learn all we could do with our new bodies, and what could be done to them?*

In sixth grade, a boy asked over Instant Messenger if I would be his girlfriend, and four hours later I called him to break it off, too nervous about what it would mean to be someone's girlfriend in person. Somewhere between fear and desire, I figured out how to take pleasure all by myself, rubbing my pelvis against the carpeted floor of my bedroom while wearing a particular pair of denim overalls. In seventh grade, my teeth chattering from Paxil, my friend Erin and I acted out the entire cast recording of *Rent*, borrowed from the library, with Barbies we both knew we were too old to play with. A couple of years later, my first kiss was in the back of a car with the best dancer at the performing arts school I attended on the weekends. He had already kissed every girl I knew, so to stand apart as someone special, I let him wrap his hands around my throat at rehearsal whenever no one was looking and squeeze. I was fascinated by the dancers because they knew already what their bodies were capable of. I was still afraid of mine. Instead of dancing, I learned to sing.

I won competitions for my performances of Mendelssohn, Bizet, Gilbert and Sullivan, and Delibes, collecting trophies for the power of my lungs. "Your voice is very . . . loud," the father of another competitor told me, inside a nave. I liked being loud. I liked hitting the sweet spot of high C, the way the note blew off the top of my head.

In public, I was a soprano, a prizewinning coquette, but home alone, I was obsessed with memorizing torch songs, laments for the unrequited love of a brute, which I downloaded off Napster. Popular in the 1920s, the torch singer was the opposite of a flapper girl. She didn't want to burn her candle at both ends; she carried only a single flame, a torch, for *dat man she can't help lovin'*. The "can't help" part is crucial. The singer is a slave to her bad romance. My favorite remains the original torch song, "My Man," sung by funny girl Fanny Brice about her shithead second husband: *What's the difference if I say I'll go away, / When I know I'll come back on my knees someday?*

❧

On our second date after the *Medea* callbacks, Jason forgot the keys to his apartment, and picked the lock with his library card. I had never dated anyone who knew how to pick a lock before. I had never dated anyone who kept a copy of *The Game: Penetrating the Secret Society of Pickup Artists* in clear display on his bookshelf either, though to be fair, there was a copy of *The Liars' Club* by Mary Karr next to it.

"You've read this?" I asked, holding up the memoir.

"Of course I have," he said, which surprised me because even though he said he'd read my poems, I still had him pegged for a semiliterate jock.

I gave myself a tour of his apartment, which I hadn't paid much attention to the first time I visited. It was a one-bedroom, for which his dad paid the rent as long as Jason went to community college. It sounded like a pretty sweet deal to me, but Jason said it was only so that his dad could get him out of the four-bedroom house he shared with his new fiancée, a ten-minute drive away.

The living room carpet was riddled with neon BB pellets. In the bedroom, he had a comforter tacked over the windows on top of the blinds to block out all light. After lots of Q&A, I'd finally figured out that Jason was only eighteen years old—but he would be turning nineteen in April, and then we'd be only three years apart, which seemed okay. My mom is three years older than my dad, a coincidence that I mentally registered as a sign.

There were no pictures of his friends or family anywhere in the apartment, only a poster of James Dean on the wall of the hallway between the living room and bedroom. Jason stood beneath it, flipped his collar, and scowled. A dead ringer.

"Have you seen *Rebel Without a Cause?*" he asked me.

"No," I said.

He promised we would watch it together.

What I loved to watch was Jason, the unselfconscious way he did the most ordinary things, like an actor in a one-man show. I studied the lines around his lips when he smoked, the grip of his hand when shifting from third to fourth gear, the square tips of his fingers when he laced his boots. When he cradled my face in his hands or kissed the inside of my elbow, it made everything in my head turn into static, white noise. He made my mind go blank. I'd never felt anything like it. And so I forgot about trying to be smart or funny or impressive—all I wanted was my body laid out like a page of Braille; I wanted Jason to read me that way.

Neither of us got cast in *Medea*, but it didn't matter. We saw each other almost every night. When I mentioned that I'd recently had my wisdom teeth out, Jason asked me to bring over my leftover pain pills and muscle relaxers. He rolled Vicodin cigarettes and we took them to the movies with us. I bought jugs of Carlo Rossi Chianti and we drank them. Matching his level of intoxication felt like part of the audition process, like this was my once-in-a-lifetime opportunity to try out for the role of the cool girl, after having always been so serious, so ambitious, so square. It was a kind of reverse ambition—what if *be whoever you want to be* meant forgetting all your dreams and having fun becoming a flop?

We stayed up so late that the suburbs turned surreal and became ours. If we had not drunk a jug of wine, we drove to the twenty-four-hour diner at two in the morning and sat in the smoking section and ate strawberry pancakes. There, he told me about the treatment facilities he'd been sent to, the detention centers, the wilderness camp in Kentucky where he'd refused to actually go outside and participate, so they'd put him in solitary confinement and he'd played "We Will Rock You" against the wall with his head for fourteen hours.

To illustrate, he began to sing the chorus while tapping his fingers on the tabletop.

"But why did you have to go to all these places?" I asked.

"Because my stepdad hated me."

Jason had grown up down south, with his mom, stepdad, and two half siblings. His dad tried to get full custody, but during the court deposition, he ruined his case by admitting that he allowed adolescent Jason to watch porn on summer visits. Jason told me that once, after his stepdad had finished beating him, Jason wrote *I HATE YOU* in his own blood on a piece of paper and put on a suit to bring it downstairs to his stepdad on a tray. Did this actually happen? I don't know. I'll never know. But I believed him, I always believed him, because of the impressive amount of detail Jason put into each of his stories. He made me feel like he'd been waiting a long time for someone like me, someone to listen to his stories with sympathy, a believer.

Snooping in Jason's medicine cabinet, I found Depakote, an antiseizure medication used to treat bipolar disorder, but when I asked about it he said doctors were constantly prescribing him medicine and nothing ever worked. The side effects always outweighed the benefits. I'd been on and off antidepressants for years, so rather than recognize a warning sign, I saw something we had in common. After Jason found my poetry online he started saying that someday he'd tell me all his stories so I could write his memoir, and then we'd both be rich.

We watched *Rebel Without a Cause*, and there he was, just as Jason wanted me to see him—in Jim Stark's blistering rage at his parents, his distant tenderness toward Natalie Wood's character Judy. From his hairline to his fingertips, Jason was James. It was uncanny. Jason also sang Johnny Cash songs with perfect pitch and slow-danced with me to "Wildwood Flower." I was falling in love with a young man who had the face of a dead movie star and the voice of a drug-addicted rebel, and so when Jason told me he usually only had sex with virgins, I asked if I could be next.

"No, then you're just going to get really attached. Believe me." The thing I couldn't believe was that he would turn down what I was asking for.

"It's not like I'm saving myself for someone," I said. "I had this boyfriend in high school for *two years* and he wouldn't do it, even though I begged him all the time."

"Sounds gay."

"Please? You'll be doing me a favor."

He looked irritated and put-upon. "Let me go see if I have any condoms," he finally said, and disappeared into the bedroom. I followed.

"Tell me your least favorite part of your body," he said, "so I'll know not to mention it."

"Do you think I should get surgery so my ears don't stick out?"

"No."

"Okay, then my legs," I said. "I hate my legs."

"Your legs are perfect."

He turned on his iPod and we kissed on the bed. The bedroom fan was on because the bedroom fan was always on, providing the white noise he needed in order to sleep. Inside the music and the whir of the blades, he was sweet and gentle until he couldn't be. With his mouth, he left bruises and crescent moons of teeth on my skin, and I loved being marked by how much he wanted me, so I could forget how much I'd begged for this. At twenty-two, my virginity was the only obstacle I could imagine that was insurmountable without another person and when I lost it I felt relief, followed swiftly by disappointment that after all this anticipation and anxiety, I didn't feel very different at all. The next morning I went home and wrote in my diary that I had lost my virginity to the song "Heartbreak Hotel."

Seven Weeks to Attract the Love of Your Life

(2007)

One morning a little less than a week later, I said I hadn't been able to fall asleep the night before and he asked why hadn't I told him—he would have hit me on the head with something hard. This was the kind of vaguely threatening thing he said to me all the time, but it didn't frighten me. It made me laugh with surprise, that instead of speaking to me like a baby, someone would address me as a sparring partner. We made plans to see each other later that evening, after he helped a girl he knew, a photography student, with a portrait project.

But I never got to see him. When I tried calling, it went straight to voice mail. My texts went unanswered. I had too much wine at dinner with my parents and went to bed with my phone, hoping a light or a vibration would wake me. Nothing. The next morning, I found the photos on Facebook of him and a Lithuanian model named Veronika—him kissing her neck, him holding her face in his hands—beside a status update to say they were "married," and then downgraded to "in a relationship."

He had mentioned that there would be a girl in the portraits with him, but I hadn't even thought through the implications of this thoroughly enough to be jealous. It was exactly fifteen days after the night I had met him. What did I expect? That I was his girlfriend? Actually, yes. Or at least that I would be soon. Seeing Veronika's face, I felt like an idiot. Of course he would choose her cheekbones, her elegant neck, her flawless skin, over mine. Clicking through the photos online again and again like a kind of self-injury, I replayed the evidence of his betrayal.

I had finally gotten my chance to play Medea: *O God, you have given to mortals a sure method / Of telling the gold that is pure from the counterfeit; / Why is there no mark engraved upon men's bodies, / By which we could know the true ones from the false ones?*

The last time I'd seen Jason, he'd held me down on the carpet and given me the worst hickey of my life, while I kicked and screamed beneath him. Now I got to wear a scarf around my neck every day, while he and Veronika did whatever it was they were doing, and wait for the bruise to fade away. I lost my appetite, and six pounds in ten days. I ran for miles along the sidewalks of my childhood, trapped in a place where everyone strived to conform and I'd spent my whole life trying to be defined by my difference. One way or another, I was going to get out of there. Good-bye, minivans. Good-bye, lawn mowers. I drove my parents' car with the moonroof up, listening to the new Arcade Fire album on repeat until I knew all the words. I cut off my hair and changed my profile picture to show off my newly prominent clavicle. I left sexual innuendos all over his Facebook wall so Veronika would see them.

If it sounds like I was often alone, that's because I was. My closest friend from childhood lived thirty minutes away with her parents, but between our work schedules, our free time rarely coincided. My other closest friends were young women I knew mostly by their usernames and avatars. In my online diary on LiveJournal, I posted about Jason, hoping for sympathy and answers: "Why did he call last night at 1:30 in the morning and not leave a message? Why do people have to die? Who the hell knows the answer to these things? I weigh less now than what I said I weighed when I lied on my driver's license."

My mom had not met Jason, but she saw the Facebook photos with Veronika and tried to convince me to move on and focus on getting into school, where I could meet my future husband. After all, that's where she met her first husband, a young Greek guy: in the multicultural club at the southern Illinois college she attended on academic scholarship in the late sixties. They moved to Chicago, and she worked full-time as a secretary while going to night school at Northwestern, eventually earning a PhD in clinical psychology. The two divorced because he wanted a wife who would run his restaurant for him, and then my mom met my dad in Evanston, where he was temporarily living at home with his parents after a breakup.

My mother is brilliant, tirelessly self-sacrificing, and determinedly optimistic. She does not complain. If you bring her a problem, she'll give you advice. After I cried to her about Jason and Veronika, she ordered a workbook off the Internet for me titled *Calling in "The One": 7 Weeks to Attract the Love of Your Life*. And then she went back to the rest of her life, which was devoted to helping people with problems worse than mine: seeing her patients, bringing groceries to the African refugee family she had adopted, tutoring children of recent immigrants in an after-school program on her day off, and visiting my disabled and mentally ill grandparents at the nursing home.

In hindsight I wonder why she couldn't just tell me it was okay to be twenty-two and single. Was it because she herself had such a hard time being alone?

I spent most of March in the grips of an obsession there seemed to be no remedy for, fueled by this idea that I was nobody if no one was in love with me. I gave up on the workbook as soon as the author said to let go of past wounds. I didn't want to; the wound was what I was most interested in. "It no longer matters why she loved her mediocre man while he was there," John Moore writes, on torch songs, "all that matters is that she loves him now he has gone."

If anything, I craved vengeance, not healing, and I wrote a poem a day on that theme. One was a poem mocking *Calling in "The One."* There was another based on a Russian folk tale about a *rusalka*, a mermaid, who loses her beloved to a foreign princess and goes to a witch for advice. The witch tells her to stab her love with a dagger—made perfect sense to me.

I sent these poems to Jason. I knew he read them late at night because I got a text at 2:40 a.m. that read, *Why do you always allude to my death in your poetry?*

When I finally got him on the phone, he explained that soon after the photography session he'd made a list of pros and cons for both me and Veronika and she was ahead by one point only because I was moving to Canada, but he still wasn't satisfied, so he flipped a coin four times and that's how he'd decided who to date.

"But I haven't even been invited for an interview yet," I said. I didn't say, to Jason or to anyone else, that if I had to choose between Canada and being his girlfriend, I would choose being his girlfriend.

"If you buy me a motorcycle, I'll dump Veronika and we can run away to Arkansas," he offered.

"I'm not buying you a motorcycle," I said, but that didn't stop me from repeating his offer—including the *dump Veronika* part—in the "favorite quotes" section of my Facebook profile and feeling triumphant when she saw it and freaked out.

"YOU HAVE TO STOP," Jason said.

Or else what?

I became irritable from not eating enough, and soon I could no longer concentrate at work. My job was to give singing lessons to children, which meant sitting all afternoon in a small windowless studio, teaching breath control to the tune of "Let's Go Fly a Kite." There was no way to check Facebook in the olden days before smartphones; the most I could do was stare at my flip phone and wait for it to buzz with a text from *dat man* who was no longer mine. I could feel myself molting like an animal—shedding my childish skin, my kindness, my passivity, and in its place growing the scales of a woman who would do anything to get what she wanted.

In a last-ditch effort to get over Jason, I posted a Craigslist personals ad, and went on a single date with a nice twentysomething who took me to the fanciest vegan restaurant in the hippest neighborhood in Chicago. Over five courses, he eagerly explained everything I never cared to know about DVD rental kiosks at grocery stores, and I failed to impress him with my accomplishments as a poet. Maybe I felt guilty that he had spent so much on dinner, knowing that I would never see him again, but I took the date's failure as a sign: I was meant to be with someone else.

After dinner I took 290 West back to the burbs, and showed up at Jason's apartment, still in my date outfit—a size-two houndstooth skirt, a royal blue blouse with a bow, and vintage kitten heels. When I'd first bought the skirt, it was too small, but thanks to him it now fit. I'd rehearsed so many dramatic love scenes in acting school that I had a script in my head for how this would go: I'd call out Jason on what he'd done, we'd argue, he'd raise his voice, I'd eventually cry, and then he'd realize what a dick he'd been and ask me back.

First I demanded to know why we weren't together.

"The sooner we start dating," he said, "the sooner we'll break up."

"But you're dating Veronika now. Does that mean you're going to break up with her soon?"

"You don't know anything about her," he said. "She was molested."

"She was *molested*?" This wasn't part of the script. "*That's* why you want to be with her instead of me?"

"That's not what I said."

In my mind, I inventoried what I had on Veronika: I was definitely thinner than her, I was probably smarter, and I was old enough to legally buy alcohol—she wasn't. Jason seemed to be enjoying the scene I was making; he was trying not to smile. I followed him around his apartment until I finally had him cornered against his kitchen counter. I leaned in to kiss him and he pulled away, laughing. I had never felt so grimly determined in my life—I was not leaving until I got back what this girl had stolen from me. I put my hand on the zipper of his jeans. He was hard.

"What are you doing?" he said.

I unzipped his pants. I went totally off script. "Cheat on Veronika," I said, "and then you'll have to be with me."

It worked. I got him back.

Shortly thereafter, Jason decided to delete his Facebook profile. He said it turned girls crazy.

❧

For Jason's nineteenth birthday, I brought stacks of quarters and did his laundry for hours. He got approved for a loan to buy a motorcycle, and took me for my first ride.

"You're going to have to hold on harder than that," he said. We rode to the gas station to get sodas.

In the parking lot he said, "I think I might be falling in love with you."

I wanted to know when he would know for certain, but decided not to push it.

Jason said I was his favorite person and called me *darling* without the *g*. We made plans to go to a water park in Wisconsin where we could hold real baby tigers. The school in Canada never even called me for an interview; I took this as another sign that we were supposed to be together, and moved into his apartment. On cold nights under the bedcovers, whenever Jason casually asked me to marry him I would say, *Sure*. When the weather got warmer, I'd sit on the grassy lip of the parking lot outside his apartment and read a book while he took his motorcycle apart and put it back together again, to see how it worked. I realized I was doing the same thing with the books I read, and told him that if I wasn't going to directing school then I wanted to write a book—a real book, a novel.

"What if we moved to New Mexico," he said, "and I could work while you wrote your novel?"

"Why New Mexico?"

"It's supposed to be a very creative place." The Land of Enchantment. Neither of us had ever been.

"Are you being serious?"

"Yeah, why not?"

"Jason," I said, "that's the most romantic thing anyone has ever said to me."

We struck a deal: six months in Albuquerque while he worked and I wrote, and then we'd move to Los Angeles and I'd work while he pursued his dream of becoming an actor.

Now we just had to tell our parents we were moving. I was excited to move but dreading the conversation with Jason and my parents. My mom had tried to help me through his betrayal and now here I was, living with him. And Jason hated to perform on command; any time he knew he was expected to make a good impression, he rebelled, grew sullen, even rude. You could never tell which Jason you were going to get. Over the course of weeks, my parents got to know the charming, hardworking Jason (they hired him to do landscaping in our backyard and he brought down most of a dead tree by swinging from it with his bare hands; he also fixed my mom's accordion with a screwdriver and she was so grateful she played "Oh! Susanna" while we danced) as well as the rude Jason, who could be surprisingly, memorably cruel.

One Saturday afternoon, Jason came with me to a state music competition, where my young students were singing and playing piano, and unsnapped my bra through my silk dress every time I turned my back on him. Humiliated in front of my students and their parents, I had to keep going in the bathroom to fix the clasp. He thought it was funny. And then he did it again at dinner, at a restaurant, in front of my own parents, and my eyes filled with tears.

"What's going on?" my mom asked.

I whispered across the table. He became instantly furious that I had "told" on him, and walked out of the restaurant. My dad, a nice guy who'd been a cool dude at CU Boulder in the early seventies, took the side of Jason, the son he never had: boys will be boys. Maybe he was right, maybe we were all overreacting to a silly prank, but my mom called out the "game" as manipulative and controlling, a way to put me in my place. She and Jason got into an argument; he accused her of raising her "feminist hackles" but promised he wouldn't do it again.

That night, after dinner, at Blockbuster, in front of one of my childhood friends working the cashier, he unsnapped my bra one last time, to see if I would say something.

I did not.

There was a part of me that didn't care what Jason did to me—hit me, bite me, hold me down, humiliate me—as long as he didn't do it in front of my parents. I didn't care if I got ruined. But I didn't think they should have to watch. I wanted to protect them more than I wanted to protect myself. Ultimately, being their daughter and being Jason's girlfriend became mutually exclusive roles, and I had to choose.

It was as if all my years of training in the performing arts had prepared me for this—not for a career onstage, but for starring in the Tennessee Williams version of my own life. At conservatory in New York, I'd played a woman cheating on her heroin-addict husband with his brother, and another woman trying to break up with

29

her married boyfriend without letting him know she was danger-ously hemorrhaging. I'd memorized that monologue from *Alcestis*, a Greek tragedy about a woman so loyal she'll sacrifice her life so her husband can keep his. I knew how to play a woman in crisis. We were both actors—Jason, too. I still have a paper he wrote on *Respect for Acting* by Uta Hagen. The section on obstacles says, "There is always an obstacle. Create one if it's not obvious."

A week or two after the music competition, we told my parents over dinner that we were heading west. My mom had the subtle yet tortured expression on her face that I recognized from times when my dad was angry and yelling, right before she usu-ally left the room to go pray. She couldn't say what it was she wanted to say.

"You don't think this is a good idea, do you?" I finally asked her.

"No," she said. "I don't."

That was the end of it. She didn't want me to go, but I was going. My dad didn't want me to go either, but he didn't want me to go anywhere. He would have been happiest if I lived at home forever. I had dropped out of high school at seventeen and moved to New York City with the help of my singing teacher on the eve of my nineteenth birthday. (I eventually got my GED in New York.) My parents knew that when I seriously committed to something, I saw it through. But what I didn't realize was that this wasn't just another one of my bold moves for independence. Moving to New Mexico was a decision I had made under the serious influence of another. *Somebody has me*, Alcestis says. *Some-body takes me away, do you see, / don't you see, to the courts / of dead men. . . . Let me go.*

After dinner, I followed Jason from my parents' house back to his apartment. He was on his motorcycle; I was driving their sedan. He sped ahead, as he always did, and I lost sight of him, until I turned down the winding tree-lined road that lead to his apartment complex, where I saw his bike stopped on the shoulder. He was talking to a police officer. I tried to catch his eyes as I drove past, to see if everything was okay, but he didn't see me.

It seemed like I waited a long time in the parking lot, but it could have been ten minutes. Finally, I saw him in my rearview mirror.

"What happened?"

"I got pulled over."

"Yeah, I saw that. Did you get a ticket?"

He was grinning. "I was speeding, but the cop had a bike, too. He wanted to know where I got mine, what year it was."

"So you did get a ticket, or you didn't?"

"You need to learn how to relax," he told me.

Niagara Falls

(2011)

I decided to go to Jason's funeral. My mom offered to drive down from Illinois and meet me in Little Rock, but I worried that if she came I'd be recast in the role of her daughter, rather than his ex-girlfriend. I already had so many conflicting feelings about meeting his mom and stepdad under these circumstances and seeing his dad again for the first time in years—the sole thing we had in common was our love of Jason, in spite of all he'd said and done to us. At the time, it didn't register that my mom was offering to come not because of her unconditional love for Jason, but because of her love for *me*.

The morning after I spoke to Jason's brother, I used Brian's laptop to go online and book a flight. Then I logged into Facebook, thinking I might post something about Jason's death so I wouldn't have to tell my friends one by one, but as soon as I signed in, I lost my train of thought. There was his face. By the time he died, Jason had deleted his Facebook profile (again) because it kept too public a record of who he was dating (made girls crazy), but nevertheless, there was his face in my feed. His best friend, Callista, had changed her profile picture to a photo of herself and Jason at prom, and when I clicked through to her friends, I entered a hall of mirrors. Jason's mom, his grandmother, his half brother—everyone had changed their profile pictures to photos of themselves with him. There he was with his family on the front porch, squinting in the sun. There he was with an ex-girlfriend, the Chicago skyline sparkling behind them. *Should I do this, too?* I wondered. I started flipping through all my Facebook albums: "Balloon Fiesta," "Leigh and Jason Go to Las Vegas," "Santa Fe," "Final Field Trip." Jason and I had lived together for a year, and known each other for another four, but in that moment I discovered there were no photos of us together.

I had twenty-six pictures I'd taken of him: in his Ray-Bans, in a fringed leather jacket, in his cowboy hat, posed beside national monuments and roadside attractions. I had a fourteen-second video of him rolling down a dune at White Sands National Monument. I had exactly two pictures of me, taken by him. But none of us together.

Were there no photos because he didn't think I was pretty? I hated myself for reverting to those familiar insecure thoughts, but my brain was determined to remind me that somewhere out there, in a place I hoped I'd never find, were the pictures of him and Veronika. I also couldn't help but remember that trip to White Sands, handing him the camera, asking him to take a picture of me near where the tall yucca stalks sprouted from the dunes. I was wearing my leather motorcycle jacket. My hair was soft and windblown. He tried for fifteen or twenty minutes to get a good shot, but in the end deleted all of them. My face just wasn't very photogenic, we decided.

I didn't change my profile picture, and I didn't post anything either. Even as someone who'd been writing online about my life since I was fifteen years old, I couldn't think of anything I wanted everyone to know—that I was devastated? Grieving? Shocked? That I was on my way to a city I'd never seen, to bury someone I loved but whom few of my friends had ever even met?

I didn't want to post publicly on Facebook or on his online memorial page, but at the same time I was desperate to be recognized as a mourner. I left Brian's company for a few hours to go back to my own apartment and pack a carry-on bag with black underwear, black sandals, and a black cotton dress.

"You don't *have* to wear all black," my mom had told me over the phone. "Funerals are more casual now."

But *all black* was a rule I could follow, even if it was self-imposed. I needed something traditional to hold on to, since I was having so much trouble navigating the territory of modern mourning: I was invisible on Facebook without a photo to share; I was mute on his memorial page. I grabbed a printed cotton shawl I'd bought in New Mexico, as if by wearing it I could wrap the entire state around me, and found the fake turquoise ring that Jason had bought me in the Ozarks. It was cheap plastic and made my ring finger sweat, but I left it on for the next week, wedding myself to my ambivalence.

Then I looked for my anxiety medication. I wanted that little orange pill bottle in my purse, just in case. Just in case *what*? I started crying and couldn't stop? I started to scream in front of people who didn't know me? It was hard to know what to expect once I got to Little Rock, but at least I could prepare for an excess of feeling. The reason I was first prescribed Ativan at all was because Jason made me see a doctor in New Mexico for acting too emotional, too "crazy."

I began searching around my desk. Since Jason had visited six weeks earlier, I hadn't slept in my own apartment once, and everything was still a mess. I'd been spending every night at Brian's luxuriously air-conditioned apartment, sleeping beside a man who was quiet and predictable and gentle. *There.* It was in the grooved part of the desk drawer where I kept my pens and pencils.

And it was empty.

Empty? The prescription had been for sixty pills, and I'd only taken a few.

Then I found a little note on my desk, written in Jason's handwriting. While I was on the phone with my boss, he'd written, *May I have an Ativan?* I must have nodded because underneath he wrote, *Thanks, you look super pretty and sound very important.* I could remember him taking a few. I could even remember him taking a few more, crushing them, and snorting them. He'd seemed manic to me that entire week, and it had taken a potent combination of pills and wine and weed to even put him to sleep for a few hours.

I couldn't fucking believe it. When I wasn't looking, he'd taken them all. I started to laugh. *Goddamnit, Jason,* I thought. *You couldn't even leave me anything to take at your funeral?*

I looked at the note again. *You look super pretty.* Maybe my face had changed a little in the years since we met—I finally had cheekbones—but what had really changed was my self-esteem.

I wasn't as insecure and desperate for his approval as I'd been at twenty-two. I'd stopped trying to be the cool girl, at the expense of everything else that mattered to me.

Still, I saved the note. A keepsake for the girl I used to be.

My bag packed, I grabbed my laptop and took the bus back to Brian's. I spent the afternoon picking out my favorite pictures of Jason: him holding a horseshoe crab at the New Mexico state fair; him pointing at me with fingers like guns at dawn in front of a sea of hot air balloons; him with his arms outstretched in the middle of a petrified lava field. Late on Sunday night, Brian walked with me to the drugstore so I could have prints made of these photos, to take with me to Little Rock, to give to his family.

"Can I see what he looked like?" Brian asked.

I showed him. When he died, Jason was twenty-three and looked just as young and golden and untouchable as he had when I met him at eighteen. Physically, he was the opposite of Brian, who was tall and lanky, his dark hair already handsomely dappled with gray at thirty-one. Brian was the *nice tall Jewish boy* my mom had been encouraging me to find for years. He was so tall he had to bend his knees when he kissed me. He was so nice it felt radical, like the time I accidentally broke two of his dinner plates and froze in the kitchen, staring at the shards on the floor, waiting for him to yell at me. Without saying anything, Brian got the dustpan from the closet and started to clean up the mess.

"You aren't mad at me?" I asked.

"It was just an accident," he said, and I went in the bedroom, shut the door, and cried along to the little voice in my head that said, *Jason would have been mad. Jason would have yelled at you.*

In so many ways, Jason and Brian were opposites (Stanley

Kowalski versus Mitch Mitchell), which was why, in the immediate aftermath of Jason's death, I imposed a gag order on myself.
I would not speak of Jason with Brian. When I showed him the
photos, I did not tell him, for example, that strangers used to
stop us in the street, to ask what movie they recognized him
from. I did not try to dredge up anecdotes that would make him
more sympathetic, like the time Jason called me from Arkansas
to tell me he'd rescued a baby squirrel that had fallen from a
tree. These were my own private bruises to poke at.

That night, while Brian slept, I went back online and lurked.
I looked at all those photos of Jason again and felt angry, bereft,
jealous, and above all, sorry for myself. I e-mailed my friend Liz in
Chicago to say, *It isn't fair.* Without any photos of us, I would never
know what we looked like as a couple. It was as if we'd never
existed. Liz wrote back:

> *The no-pics thing is sad, but I think it speaks to your
> closeness with him. That's the way it goes with the people
> who are the closest or most comfy together. You never have
> pictures together b/c you see each other all the time. It's like
> somebody having pictures of Niagara Falls but none of
> their hometown. Niagara is a one-time attraction. Home
> is home.*

El Chupacabra

(2007)

We left for New Mexico on a Sunday afternoon less than six months after we'd met. The plan was to drive straight through, from Chicago to Amarillo, because he wanted to spend the night in Texas, and I was willing to give him what he wanted. We rented a twenty-two-foot-long truck and we filled it with everything we owned—hundreds of books, boxes of clothes, a dining room table, a bed, and his motorcycle. To the back, we hitched Jason's Mazda.

For nineteen hours, Jason drove and I navigated from a printed map. Neither of us slept. There was supposed to be a meteor shower that night, but industrial light pollution in southern Illinois obscured the horizon, and then a thunderstorm shook the sky in St. Louis. Maybe missing the peak of the Perseids was the opposite of an auspicious sign, but we drove on.

In Cuba, Missouri, we stopped at a gas station hung with an old Coke facade to buy energy drinks, and a fluorescent green June beetle crawled over my sandaled foot. I weighed whether or not I should be afraid. In the weeks leading up to our departure, Jason had been waking me up in the middle of the night to scare me with realistic-looking photographs of mythical or extinct creatures of the southwestern United States that he'd found on the Internet. *This is* el chupacabra. *And this is a teratorn, a huge bird of prey. You'll find them both in the Land of Enchantment.*

By dawn, we were in Oklahoma. As the sun rose over the Sooner State, there were weeds and cottonwoods and DO NOT DRIVE THROUGH SMOKE signs all along I-44, and we wondered what could be burning along a highway with so few exits. In Vinita, we stopped for breakfast at what was advertised to be the largest McDonald's in the world, and were disappointed to find it was just a huge highway overpass spanning the Will Rogers Turnpike. Back in the truck, even with the air-conditioning on, we were sweaty and delirious from fast food and sleep deprivation. As if to beckon Texas to us, Jason started playing "La Grange" off his ZZ Top *Greatest Hits* CD on repeat. Every time the song ended, it was my job to hit "back" and suffer through another bass line intro.

"I keep seeing these huge birds," he said.

"What birds?" Was this another one of his signature impressions? Johnny Depp as Hunter S. Thompson in *Fear and Loathing in Las Vegas*?

Jason laughed and shook the birds from his head. Took his fake Ray-Bans off and put them on again. Hit the steering wheel in time to Billy Gibbons's laughter: *Uh-huh-huh-huh-huh.*

I never got to drive the truck for the same reason that I never got to sleep in the passenger seat: he wouldn't allow it. I'd paid for the truck, but if I somehow got us into an accident, it would be my fault, and if I dozed off it might make him doze off and get us into an accident, and then, too, Jason said, the fault would be mine. I had to stay awake.

Jason's dad called when we were still in Oklahoma and, once he heard our voices, suggested we pull over at a rest stop and take a nap. We promised we would, which was just a lie to get off the phone, and kept on driving.

Finally: Amarillo, though it was hard to know we'd even arrived. I said, "This place looks like a drunk decided to build a highway over a steakhouse and call it a day." Not that I cared where we stopped. If I had to listen to "La Grange" one more time, I'd throw my body from the cab. We parked the truck, checked into the hotel, showered, pulled the drapes against the sun, and had the kind of sex that is a deliberate, familiar invitation to sleep.

Later, at dinner, we asked our Chili's waiter what there was to do for fun.

"There isn't anything to do here."

"But what do you and your friends do on a Friday night?" Jason asked.

"Drive to Albuquerque," he said, "and get drunk." Albuquerque was four hours away.

On our way out of town the next morning, we got cowboy hats, and just inside the New Mexico state border, I bought rattlesnake-fang earrings and decided that they would bring me luck. In forty-eight hours, we'd crossed the plains, and now the arid landscape spread before us, all ochre hills and boundless bright blue sky, promising we would get what we'd come for: a life unlike the one we'd been living. The apartment we'd found on the Internet was clean and bright and new. Washer and dryer in unit. Hundreds of miles away from our parents, we were adults now. We thought being adults meant doing whatever we wanted, including to ourselves, to each other.

While we were signing our new lease, the women in the rental office asked what had brought us to New Mexico. I said I wanted to write a book and he said he wanted "to find *el chupacabra*"; somehow his answer seemed more realistic to them than mine. So Jason and the landlord shook on a deal: if he found *el chupacabra*, and brought her the head, we could live there rent-free.

In Albuquerque in August, the temperature hovers in the upper eighties during the day, but the nights are cool and starlit. For the first couple of weeks, Jason looked for a job and we both tried to adapt to the new climate and elevation by following advice I'd read on the Internet that said to drink an ounce of water for every pound you weighed. The Sandia Mountains, named for their watermelon-colored glow, towered dramatically out our eastern-facing windows, casting a rosy shadow over a sprawling city of terra-cotta and turquoise, midcentury motels and homeless hippies, fast-food drive-throughs and parking lots filled with model mobile homes, and strip malls stuck in the middle of high desert beauty. As it cooled toward dusk, we'd put on the cowboy hats we'd bought in Amarillo and go out to the rocky ditch across the road to shoot BB guns at Sprite cans. I wasn't a very good shot, but I was impressed with the idea of myself standing there, holding Jason's gun, taking aim.

Then we'd walk back across the road, open a fifth of gin, and start the grill for dinner. One evening, as we were checking the vegetables to see if they were done, we met our neighbor Jimmy, who told us he was forty-seven but looked closer to sixty. He was a few inches shorter than me; I could watch myself talk to him in his blue reflective sunglasses. Jason said we'd moved here so I could write a book and then we were going to go to LA so he could be an actor, and so Jimmy started calling Jason "Hollywood." I didn't get a nickname. He invited us to a party that night in the apartment complex next to our own, and after a couple of hours of drinking Tecate and watching Ultimate Fighting on TV, we watched Jimmy snort cocaine off the dining room table.

A guy named Rico asked us why we'd moved there. "To have an adventure," Jason said.

Rico laughed at us. "People come here going, 'Look at the pretty sagebrush,'" he said, "but we call it weeds."

Out on the balcony, Rico showed me a video of an Iraqi decapitation he had saved on his cell phone, for no apparent reason. Jimmy approached on my other side. "Me and Rico had a threesome with Mandy," he whispered. This was Mandy's apartment.

"Oh," I said.

"She likes girls, too. All the girls are bi in New Mexico. I can ask her for you, if you want me to."

"Ask her what?" I said.

I went to go find Jason. "Don't leave me alone with Jimmy," I said, but he wasn't listening.

When Jason ran out of cigarettes, Jimmy insisted on driving us to Walgreens himself, and I sat on Jason's lap in the front of the truck so I wouldn't have to sit between them. Jimmy kept his blue sunglasses on, even in the dark. On the way out of the parking lot, he hit a mailbox and busted one of the side mirrors on his truck.

I wasn't afraid of riding in a car with someone who probably shouldn't have been driving it. I was tallying it up as another adventure, a future story to tell about one of the many things I should not have done but did.

Jimmy disappeared from the party soon after we got back, claiming his girlfriend would be mad at him for damaging the truck, and I tried to imagine what this girlfriend might look like. The six of us left—Rico, Mandy, Jason, and I, and a married couple whom Jason had caught having sex on the floor of Mandy's bathroom earlier that night—hopped the locked fence to the swimming pool and took off our clothes. Treading water in our underwear, no one had much to say, and through the pool's blue surface my legs were pale and spectral.

In the years after we finally broke up, Jason and I developed a shorthand for revisiting nights like those. On long-distance calls I would ask, "Remember the night we rode in Jimmy's truck and he broke the mirror? Remember when we hopped the fence to go swimming? Remember Amarillo, how tired we were?"

He always answered the same way: "Of course I remember."

And I always felt relief when he said it. The stories he confirmed for me were always the memories I trusted the most, because my partner in crime had admitted to being at the scene.

Once he was gone, I was the only one left to remember.

Shortly after Jason died, I watched a documentary about the Mayans on TV. As the narrator was explaining their ancient visual language, the glyph for the word *conjuring* appeared on screen. It showed two hands trying to grab a fish. In a notebook, I scribbled, *Mayan glyph for* conjuring *shows two hands trying to grab a fish*. I didn't know why I had to write it down, but I couldn't shake the image from my mind. Was I a conjurer? Of what? Months later, I would find my own note and realize that without Jason, my memories were fish. I couldn't hold them. I didn't *trust myself* to hold them. Without someone to verify and say, *I was there, too*, I didn't believe that any of my experiences were real. They slipped from my hands as soon as I got a grip.

At a desk that faced the Sandias, I wrote every day, on an Acer laptop I'd bought from a friend for $175. When the guy came to install our cable and phone, he told us the mountains weren't all natural formations. "The government built some of that to look like mountains," he said. "To hide the missiles."

"No," I said, disbelieving.

"Ask anyone. If there's a nuclear attack on America? Albuquerque's where they'll target. New Mexico's where all the secrets are."

Our apartment complex was very close to Kirtland Air Force Base, and we'd seen strange aircraft overhead, like misshapen helicopters or miniature Hindenburgs. Every day, I saw an old hippie in a bucket hat, standing on the side of the road with a sign that read WORK FOR PEACE, trying single-handedly to convince all the bright minds who worked on the base to do something else.

I told our neighbor José what the cable guy had said, about the mountains being a false front, one night when we were in the hot tub at the apartment complex. José said he'd heard that, too.

"Have you ever seen *el chupacabra*?" Jason asked.

José laughed but didn't deny its existence. "No, but in high school my buddies and me were out one night and we saw La Llorona down along the Rio Grande. Scared us to death."

All the variations of the story of La Llorona, the Weeping Woman, begin with a poor, beautiful young woman. In one version, she has an affair with a rich, handsome man and bears him three children. The man eventually leaves her to marry another woman, someone of his own higher class. Grief-stricken and furious, the young woman takes her children to the river and drowns them. And then she kills herself.

At the gates of heaven, God asks her where her children are. She says she doesn't know. He sends her back to earth, to roam the river until she finds them. Only then will he allow her to enter heaven. People who believe in the myth say she still wanders the banks, crying.

"What did she look like?" I asked José, imagining a woman with long black hair, dressed all in white.

"She was dressed all in white," he said, and I believed him.

The Girls

(2007)

Out in this desert we are testing bombs,
that's why we came here.

ADRIENNE RICH, "TRYING TO
TALK WITH A MAN"

I didn't know how to drive the only car we'd brought with us. It was a Mazda Protege, black, with 133,000 miles and a manual transmission. All summer long, before we moved, Jason had promised to teach me how to use the clutch and shift gears, but he never did. There were plenty of reasons why he didn't: I might wreck it; I wasn't on his insurance; he needed the car more than I did. The Mazda was a gift from his dad's new girlfriend—it was her old car and though it was not exactly a piece of shit, Jason expressed how he felt about their relationship by treating it like one.

My new life was circumscribed by the places to which I could walk (the swimming pool, the mailbox) and the places he was willing to drive us to (the twenty-four-hour Walmart). A few times a week I filled a shopping bag with empty Sprite cans and gin bottles and cereal boxes and walked to the recycling center. One day, as I was lobbing cans over the side of a Dumpster, an elderly woman stopped and asked where I was from.

"From Illinois," I said.

"What brings you to New Mexico?"

"I'm here with my boyfriend."

Her eyes sparkled. "Going to get married?"

I could have said, *I don't know yet; first I have to finish the novel I'm writing*, but instead I just smiled and nodded, pulling a happy ending out of the thin blue air like a rabbit from a hat.

Jason was hired to work maintenance at our apartment complex, and in the mornings I got up earlier than him, to start the coffee and make bacon and eggs. I was happy to have a routine, happy to play the housewife as long as he kept up his side of the bargain: holding a job while I wrote my book. After breakfast, he walked over to the main office and hopped in the golf cart he got to drive around all day and I took my coffee over to my desk and checked my word count from the day before. I tried to write at least a thousand words a day, and I wrote like mad in the mornings, trying to get in as many words as I could before Jason pulled up in his golf cart for lunch. I'd make him a grilled cheese and he'd pour himself a gin and tonic.

"Since you don't need the car during the day . . . maybe you could teach me how to drive and I could go somewhere."

"Where would you go?"

"I don't know," I said. We had been there only a few weeks and I hadn't seen enough of Albuquerque to even know what my options were. I felt like a prisoner who was unable to tell her jailer what she would do once she was released.

"You're supposed to be writing a book," he reminded me. "You don't need to go anywhere to write a book."

After he went back to work, I'd try to reenter the world of my

characters, but it was difficult—there were always afternoon inter-
ruptions. Jason would call to say he'd argued with a coworker, or
with a resident. Something about a lightbulb, a doorjamb, a sink
plug. Everyone but him was incompetent, an asshole. "Sucks," I'd
say. "Uh-huh, uh-huh." He said he wanted to quit. I said he
couldn't quit; he'd *promised* to work while I wrote. Before we'd
left, my mom had warned me that Jason seemed to be built of
promises, but I still believed him because I was his believer, the
one person in his life willing to give him the benefit of the doubt.

By the time he got off work, I'd be itching to go out and he'd
be too tired to move. Either we'd drink gin and tonics until we
lost track of what number we were on, or we'd get high instead.
Then he'd drive us to the Walmart, which we treated like our
own private amusement park. I rode the coin-operated toddler
rides by the front door, and Jason rode a motorized shopping cart
and had me walk beside him, to verify that he was disabled if an
employee asked (they did). We bought liquor and frozen apple
pies. We spent a long time watching the Venus flytraps in action in
Home and Garden.

One night, while I was standing in the checkout line, my
dad called my cell phone. "How's the Southwest?" he asked.

"Good," I said.

"I bet you've been seeing a lot of amazing stuff out there."

I closed my eyes. I tried to think of one amazing thing I
could tell my dad about—it didn't even have to be amazing, it
just had to be *something*. But when I flipped through the catalog
of my memory of the past few weeks, there was nothing but the
fluorescent interiors of chain stores and the view of the TV from
the couch.

"The mountains," I sputtered. "I can see the mountains from my desk when I write." Then I started to cry and said I had to go. I could barely get through the transaction with the checkout lady; I felt my chest contract like a fist and my peripheral vision disappeared. Through a tunnel of light, I somehow made it out to the car, where Jason was waiting for me.

"I think I'm having a panic attack," I said, sobbing.

"Why?"

"We never go anywhere! I'm stuck here!"

"Well, I feel stuck, too!" he said. "Do you think this is what I want to do, just go to work every day while you get to write your book?"

I cried harder. He promised we would see more, do more—the New Mexico State Fair, the balloon fiesta in October, Santa Fe—if he could have something to look forward to himself. When we got home, Jason went online and found that the University of New Mexico was holding auditions for a musical. At the time it didn't occur to me that if he got cast I would be home alone even more often; I only made him promise he would keep his maintenance job.

Jason memorized a monologue he found on the Internet and performed it in our living room; it was from the perspective of a young man who'd lost his girlfriend in an accident and how he would always remember her brown eyes. On paper, I thought it was cheesy and sentimental, but when he performed it, it was sad and haunting.

"You'll get it," I said, and I was right. He was cast as one of the leads.

Now, every night after work, he put on his jacket and rode his bike to rehearsal, while I sat at home, e-mailing friends, writing love poems. He always came home flushed and manic, with something to brag about. Everyone at UNM loved him, he said. I wanted to be happy for him, that he had a chance to do what he was good at, but then Jason blurted out that after dating me for *so long* (between five and seven months, depending on which of us was counting), meeting new girls was like opening presents at Christmas.

"What does that mean?" I said. "You want to fuck them?"

"They want to fuck me." *But I want to fuck you*, I thought but didn't say. We were having sex less and less. He never initiated anymore, and if I tried, he would tell me, "It's not sexy when you beg."

I would never meet any of these UNM girls, but they loomed large in my imagination: the enemy.

"What *are* they?" I finally asked him, by which I meant, *What are they that I am not?*

They were dancers. To compete, I found a regimen on a cheerleading website that promised to teach me to do full splits in fifteen minutes a day. I dyed my hair red in the bathroom sink. I took up smoking. Thinking I still might lose him to one of *them*, I offered the idea of a threesome, and even went online to browse for a girl we could invite over some night. *I'm 140 pounds*, one of the ads said, *but I keep it tight*. There was a picture of her from the neck down, wearing a bra and underwear. We never contacted her, but I continued grooming myself, as if training for a sexiness war. Every morning in the shower I shaved my legs, my armpits, the tiny soft hairs under my navel, and then everything between my legs, because he wouldn't touch me otherwise. Sometimes Jason pulled the curtain back, just to look at me. Other times he came into the bathroom just to watch me pee. I called this lack of privacy "intimacy." At night we slept back-to-back, butts touching, like two opposing archery bows.

When we left for Albuquerque, our parents gave us parting gifts. From Jason's dad, Victor: a gold necklace with Jesus on the cross for Jason and two cookbooks and a clothbound diary for me. From my mom: another cookbook, with color photos of how to truss a turkey, and two self-help books, *Transforming Anxiety: The HeartMath Solution for Overcoming Fear and Worry and Creating Serenity* and *Transforming Anger: The HeartMath Solution for Letting Go of Rage, Frustration, and Irritation*. From my dad: fifty bucks to give anyone we could find to help us unload our furniture from the truck. (When I tried to give this money to our new neighbors Ted and Diane, who helped us carry our bed into the apartment, they politely refused to accept it.)

The first entry in the diary describes our road trip to New Mexico. The fourth entry, from two weeks later, begins *I don't feel safe with myself.* Only on these private pages could I record all the things I was too ashamed to admit to anyone: how much I was drinking, how sick I felt. *I feel as if this was a mistake. Maybe we were meant to meet and know each other, but this is all too much. I haven't told him this, but I worry I'd sleep with some other guy and he'd convince me to end it with Jason because I deserve better.*

What's hard to understand, but what I know to have been true, is that I was more afraid that someone would successfully convince me to leave Jason than I was of staying with him.

In e-mails to friends I was always carefully measuring what

to leave in (I craved sympathy and understanding) and what to leave out (I couldn't tolerate being told I deserved better, even if I knew it myself, because that meant I was choosing to stay inside the nightmare, and therefore everything he did was the consequence of my not leaving). To my friend Julia in New York, who asked, *How is the west? Tell me absolutely everything*, I replied with a list of the good and the bad. The good: the weather, the mountains, the food, the fact that I was running and writing every day. The bad: I couldn't drive, we didn't go anywhere, and:

> *Sometimes I feel like we are best friends who sleep in the same bed and then I feel bad that we aren't in a romantic relationship. Sometimes I feel like we are in a romantic relationship, but it is a bad, abusive kind that I should get out of. For example, sometimes we roughhouse and wrestle a little bit, but it's turned into him hitting my legs or my arms sometimes out of anger, and not HARD, but a play slap out of anger is different than a play slap. He hit my arm in Walmart and it hurt so bad I started to cry and then he got mad at me for crying. See? This is abusive and I recognize that and I try to talk to him about it and he tells me I'm always playing the victim.*

I left out the part where a couple passed by us at Walmart, after he had hit my arm, and Jason hissed in my ear to stop crying, "or else they'll think I hit you." I left out the part where he threw me against the refrigerator and didn't believe how badly I said I was hurt until he lifted my shirt and saw the bruises on my back.

Then, remorseful, he left me alone the next time he was mad and only punched a hole through our bathroom door. *I hope this e-mail isn't coming off like a cry for help*, I wrote to Julia. *It's hard to be really honest. I'm not unhappy and you shouldn't worry.*

In the *Albuquerque Journal* "Help Wanted" section, I found a listing for a diner in need of waitresses. I checked the address online, and it was a little less than two miles away. The nearest bus only came once an hour, but that was okay: I could walk. I'd walked all over Chicago and all over New York. Forget learning to drive, or asking Jason for a ride. I would walk all over Albuquerque, too.

It was approaching a hundred degrees when I left the apartment, hiked up the frontage road to Eubank, and made a right. For interview attire, I'd picked a strapless black cotton dress, meant to be a swimsuit cover-up, because it wouldn't show the sweat, and pink plastic jelly sandals. I crossed Central Avenue, the old Route 66, and walked another mile and a half, past the Walmart and Del Taco, and over I-40. A man on a bike asked if I wanted a beer. Cars honked. Some drivers stopped to ask if I wanted a ride. When I ignored them and kept walking, they peeled away, blowing dirt and gravel in their wake, scratching my bare legs. I passed no other pedestrians.

A dry heat. That was the number one thing people told us about the Southwest, before we moved there. But it's hard to even imagine what dry heat feels like if you've only known humidity. Humidity is ubiquitous and punishing, but at least a dry heat cools in the shade. By the time I arrived at the restaurant, I was hot but not melting.

I'd brought a résumé with me, of my past restaurant experience working as a hostess in Chicago and a coat-check girl in New York, but I still had to fill out a photocopied application. Warren, the manager, hired me on the spot to hostess until I could take a legally required licensing exam to serve alcohol in the state of New Mexico, and then I could wait tables. I was supposed to go buy black pants and, eventually, a black apron for my uniform. From the glass case under the front register, Warren pulled a white T-shirt with an owl and a Route 66 sign on it. He and all the other middle-aged managers were men. All the waitresses were women, whom the managers called *girls*; the hostesses were girls, too, and the busboys were boys.

It was a Friday. I was supposed to start on Sunday, during the breakfast shift.

On Saturday, I bought black pants and then spent the rest of the afternoon stretched out by the pool in my red bikini, getting sun and reading my book about overcoming anxiety. I was feeling warm and fine. I was feeling like a champ at overcoming: I had a boyfriend, an apartment, a job, a novel in progress, and I was a few days closer to my goal of the full splits. A dad was in the pool with two little girls wearing matching lavender swimsuits with built-in inner tubes. He tossed the girls in the air and they came splashing back down, asking to be thrown again as soon as they hit the water.

That night, Jason said he was going to a party and I wasn't allowed to come.

"Why not?"

"You have to let me have a life," he said. "These are my friends."

I'd never told him this, but one of the perks of being his girlfriend was getting to go places with him and be seen at the side of someone with so much charisma. I liked the way other women looked at me. I liked knowing I had something that they did not. I couldn't think of anything I'd had before worth envying.

I practiced taking the deep breaths I'd just read about by the pool, and told him I wouldn't be able to fall asleep without him.

He said he would roll me a joint.

But I couldn't imagine smoking out this anxiety; all I could do was imagine, on repeat, him fucking one of his new Christmas presents while I sat at home, alone. I started to beg, but this just reinforced why he didn't want me there: I was boring; I was a nag; I was not sexy. When I started to cry, he pointed out that he couldn't show up to a party with a girl who was crying.

After he left, I called my mom and surrendered. I didn't say she was right, I never should have moved to Albuquerque with him. I didn't admit that he had slapped me and thrown me against the fridge, but I did tell her he wanted to see other people and that I had exhausted every strategy in the *Transforming Anxiety* book she'd given me. At this point, I needed more than a book. I needed a mother, and mine was a professional at helping people in crisis. She never gasped or yelled or cried. In the same calm voice I'd heard her use behind closed doors, on the phone with suicidal patients, she told me exactly what to do, and I did it, relieved to have directions to follow.

Using what was left of my savings after all of our moving expenses, I bought a one-way plane ticket. I packed a suitcase. I wrote a letter that began, *Dear Jason, This isn't working for me. I'm flying to Chicago*, and left it on the coffee table, placing the joint and the lighter on top like paperweights. I called a taxi to take me to the Wyndham Hotel near the airport, where I could spend the night before my flight left the next morning. I turned off my cell phone so he couldn't reach me if he tried, and promised to call my mom back from the landline in my hotel room.

A shitty Checker cab with ruptured vinyl seats showed up and the driver wanted to talk. "There isn't anything to do in this town except go to the liquor store," he said, "am I right?" I didn't want to talk. I just wanted to stare out the window and memorize each terra-cotta-and-turquoise underpass on the highway. The night was cool, and the sky was punctured with stars. I was sitting on my shaking hands, murmuring, "Yeah. Uh-huh. I know what you mean."

"A bunch of alcoholics," he continued. "Everyone's an alcoholic."

At the Wyndham, the first room key they gave me didn't work. Neither did the second. On my third trip to the front desk, I had to make small talk in the elevator with a middle-aged couple from New Zealand, and I could feel myself split in two: one of me was recounting the tragedy of the faulty room key, and the other me was numb and floating away on an irreversible course, like a hot air balloon about to crash into electrical wires.

I spent the night on the phone talking to my parents, afraid to sleep and afraid that Jason would, somehow, find me. "Love is as love does," my mom said, and I wrote this on the hotel notepad by the phone. All my dad could think to suggest was a hot bath, and so when I finally hung up the phone, I ran the water and soaked in the deep tub. I realized that for the first night in a long time, I was sober.

❧

Four weeks to the day after we'd left Illinois for New Mexico, my plane touched down at Midway. I turned my cell phone on while we taxied to the terminal and listened to nine voice mails from Jason. He wanted to know where I was. He wanted to know how I could do this to him. "I'm drunk, I just drank a lot of NyQuil, I went over to Ted and Diane's to see if you're there, but you're not." He hadn't believed what I wrote in my letter, that I really had flown back to Chicago.

My mom picked me up at baggage claim and even though I'd followed her advice to the letter, I'd never seen her less happy to see me. I hadn't called Jason back yet because I wanted to do it in front of a witness, but I didn't know what I wanted the witness to do while I called. Did I want her to make reassuring facial expressions? Did I want her to be there in case I cracked, so she could take the phone from my hand? What would that mean, to "crack"? Was I afraid that I would apologize for leaving? The fact that I'd physically gotten away from Jason didn't prevent all my thoughts from orbiting around him, like planets around the sun.

She watched me while I called him back.

He answered immediately: "Where are you?"

"I told you where I am. I'm in Chicago."

"I'm leaving right now, and I'm coming to get you."

"In the car?"

"The motorcycle."

I received these words as proof of his devotion. *Good idea*, I thought. *Come and get me.* I put my hand over the mouthpiece.

"He says he's going to come pick me up on his motorcycle," I told my mom, expecting her to be excited about this new development.

"Hang up the phone," she said.

I felt stunned and confused, unable to understand why she was being so cold when I was in such agony. Even though I'd gone through all the actions of leaving Jason, I couldn't imagine staying away from him for good. Didn't she know that? Hadn't I just flown across the country so that he would realize he wanted me back? I did what she told me to do—I left my phone off all night, and hadn't he learned his lesson now? Wasn't she on my side? Wasn't this what we both wanted? It did not occur to me that she and I wanted completely different outcomes.

"I'll have to call you back later," I told Jason, even though a part of me wondered if later would be too late: if he would already be on his motorcycle, flying down the highway, coming to get me.

We picked up my suitcase from the baggage carousel (I had packed two dozen books I thought I might need until I got back home to Albuquerque) and went to the parking garage.

"I forgot how ugly the sky is here," I said, like a petulant child, once we were on the tollway. I was slumped in the passenger seat; I hadn't driven a car in weeks. The blue horizon was divided by billboard ads: cell phone company, pizza place, strip club, strip club.

"Is it really so different?"

Yes. I'd been to Mars and back.

For the next twenty-four hours I lay on the trampoline in my parents' backyard, soaking up sun, making phone calls. I called Julia. I called back our neighbor Diane, who'd left a message to see if I was okay. I cringed every time I pictured Jason arriving at her door on Saturday night, drunk, looking for me, and tried to come up with a believable explanation for why I'd run away, without mentioning the threat of other women, or him hitting me.

"It's just that sometimes he drinks too much and we get into fights and this seemed like the only way to get through to him," I said.

"If you're concerned about how much he's drinking," she said gently, "then maybe don't buy him alcohol."

I felt embarrassed at being chided, and wanted to defend myself, but had no good argument. By trying to absolve Jason, I'd implicated myself. I was the enabler. I was the one who stood in line at Walmart or Walgreens with ID ready while Jason hovered in the background, playing with the whirligigs placed to entice children at the checkout.

"You're right," I told Diane. "I know you're right."

I called Jason.

"You betrayed me," he said. "I've been throwing up all day and drinking gin. I thought you loved me.

"Everyone I've ever loved has abandoned me," he reminded me, and started to cry.

If I didn't come back, he said he would take all my books out to the parking lot and burn them.

I remember nothing of my side of the conversation. I must have kept trying to explain how miserable I was until it seemed like finally he heard me, and changed his tune to one of remorse. "I'm sorry," he said. "We need to work on this. I love you. I want you to tell me why you're depressed. I think you're so smart, and my dad says I should get down on my knees every day and thank God I have you."

I knew what the cycle of abuse was, I knew the highs and the lows, and I could recognize that Jason's remorse and promises were what drew me back into his web. But wasn't he right? Wasn't I so smart? So smart that I could see exactly what I was doing in making a choice to go back to him? If we could just work on this, I thought, we could show everyone that our move wasn't a mistake, that I wasn't a victim of anything—Jason and I could prove we really were as special as we felt ourselves to be.

My parents tried to get me to at least stay the week, to make him sweat it out in Albuquerque and really miss me. At least that's what they said. It would be years before I understood that my parents had thought that by coming home I'd finally become strong enough to leave him. Like when we moved to New Mexico in the first place, my mom felt, as much as she didn't want me to go, that this was my life, my decision.

I was home for only twenty-four hours.

Over the phone, Jason and I reached an agreement: he would teach me how to drive stick, he wouldn't sleep with other people, he would stop teasing (hitting) me. In return, I had to go back on antidepressants for the first time in years so I would stop acting "crazy." He promised to pick me up at the airport Monday night. I called Warren and apologized for missing my first day of work, but there was a "family emergency," and he said I could start on Tuesday, but it couldn't happen again. I didn't tell him I was calling from thirteen hundred miles away.

Because there were no psychiatrists who could see me for at least six weeks, I made an appointment with a general practitioner, and

Jason and I took the car to the gravelly frontage road near our apartment for my first driving lesson. I hardly ever saw any other vehicles use it, and I wasn't even sure where it led. Jason claimed that he rode his bike to the end of the road one night while I was sleeping and reached some militarized no-trespassing zone. An armed guard told him to turn around and go back.

To the east rose the Sandias, jagged and rosy.

To the west, overlooking the mountains, sat a school for the blind.

Jason and I walked around the car, switching places so I could take the driver's seat. A woman in her sixties passed on a scooter, wearing a helmet and a pair of shades. She looked tan and happy.

"I love your scooter!" I shouted.

She waved at us and rode by.

"When we move to LA, we'll get you a scooter," Jason promised. Oh good. He still wanted to move to LA with me. Maybe Albuquerque was just an endurance test before our real life could start in Hollywood.

"Really? Is it hard to ride?"

"No," he said, "it's really easy."

Really easy, just like driving his car was supposed to be, once he'd explained the clutch and gearshift. How would I know when to switch gears? You pay attention to the RPM. *What's RPM?* I wondered, but didn't ask because it sounded like something I was already supposed to know. What gear should I put it in when I start the car? You don't put it in gear; you leave it in neutral.

I started the ignition. So far, so good.

I shifted into first, and we lurched ahead. There was a horrible grating sound. I was doing something wrong. The car stalled. I had to start over again. I couldn't get the hang of coordinating the clutch, the gas, and the gearshift. By the time I graduated from first to second gear, Jason was too frustrated with me to continue the lesson; I got the sense that driving stick was something you either had a natural talent for or you didn't, and I did not. He made me get out and sit in the passenger seat. We went home. This lesson would be my first and my last with him, though eventually our neighbor Diane took me to a nearby parking lot and taught me to shift gears in her truck. Jason didn't want me back in the driver's seat of his car until I could actually drive.

The first place I drove myself to was the library. To get there, I had to go uphill on Tramway. I got anxious at stoplights because it was hard for me to accelerate uphill without stalling. I took the bus when I went to see the general practitioner about my panic attacks.

"About how many panic attacks are you having?"

"Six or seven a week," I said.

He didn't believe me, even when I described the symptoms: it felt like I would never be able to stop crying, it felt like being choked, it felt like some big man was sitting on my heart. He wrote me a prescription for Zoloft and ten Ativans, with the warning that they could be addictive. He asked what had brought me to New Mexico, and this time I didn't say *to write a book*, or *to have an adventure*. I said, "My boyfriend."

He asked how old my boyfriend was.

"Nineteen," I told him.

"He's still young," he said. "You gotta give him a break."

Along with the ten Ativans, he recommended we drive north up into the mountains to see the leaves change from green to gold.

The Sylvia Plath Effect
(1998)

I know the bottom, she says. I know it with
my great tap root:
   It is what you fear.
   I do not fear it: I have been there.

SYLVIA PLATH, "ELM"

Picture of me at thirteen: dark, naturally curly hair out of nowhere (in a couple of years it will be straight again), broad shoulders, arms like reeds, mouth pursed to hide two rows of crooked teeth. In a Polaroid, I'm sitting on the wooden ladder that goes with the playhouse in our backyard, wearing a teal cotton tank top with a butterfly embroidered near the neckline. I have already started to pluck my eyebrows, so they look under control, but my eyes seem weirdly wide set, and my mouth is puffy. My face is still growing. I'm squinting at the soft light that filters through the maple leaves. It's spring: suicide weather.

This photo was taken so I would have a picture of myself to send to Daniel, my friend in Las Vegas. We'd met on a message board for Andrew Lloyd Webber fans and talked every day, either online, or by phone, long-distance. I paid for the charges with my babysitting money. Sometimes my dad would eavesdrop on our calls because he was suspicious of Daniel's baritone, but there was nothing dangerous or inappropriate about our relationship. Daniel was exactly who he said he was—a middle schooler, a Mormon, a fan of *Starlight Express* and Peanuts cartoons. We had our own AOL screen names but no digital cameras, no scanners. Using *Beauty and the Beast* stationery from the Disney Store, Daniel mailed me a letter and a photo of what he looked like: tall, lanky, exceptionally tan. I was supposed to send him my picture in return.

But I never sent him my photo, because I was sick that spring. I got headaches frequently, and convinced my parents to let me stay home from school by myself two or three days a week. I slept through the school day, and resented my dad, who called me every few hours from his corporate desk job to see how I was feeling. *Bad. Fine. Tired.* These calls were routine and always followed the same script; I'd give my answers in monotone and he'd end the conversation by suggesting I go drink some ginger ale.

My mom took me to a chiropractor, who discovered two compressed vertebrae in my cervical spine. (She thinks that they became compressed during birth because she tried for so many hours to deliver me vaginally before she finally agreed to have a C-section.) The X-ray they took of my neck fascinated me. Next to an X-ray of a "normal" spine, it was obvious what was wrong with mine. Where there should have been space, there was none. When I stood on two scales in their office (one foot on each), I weighed fifteen pounds more on one side than the other. I was crooked. If I came for treatment two or three times a week, they said they could fix me.

But the ache in my head was more than just a symptom of a

misaligned spine. I heard voices. They'd begun when I was about four, and that spring when I was thirteen, they reached a climactic pitch. The voices were louder and came more frequently than ever before. I wasn't afraid of them, but their arrival was always physically uncomfortable and mentally exhausting. First I'd feel a distinctive pulling sensation, like one part of my brain detaching from the other. Then there'd be cotton in my ears, silencing the sounds outside my head, so that I could hear what was inside: a chorus of voices, adult men and women, telling me how bad I was. I sat still and listened, paralyzed, until they went away on their own and I could fall back asleep.

Since I was in the habit of sleeping all day, I was up all night, wracked with sadness. Sometimes I couldn't stop crying and other times I couldn't start. I copied Sylvia Plath poems, by hand, into a notebook. There was a lot in her poems I didn't understand, but when I read the lines quietly to myself, I heard the voice of someone whose head was under siege in the same way mine was. *I am terrified by this dark thing / That sleeps in me; / All day I feel its soft, feathery turnings, its malignity.* I looked up *malignity* in the dictionary. It meant *wishing evil to others*. My depression, my headaches, my voices—these were all malignant. I was their victim, but I didn't know how to fight back because I never could tell if the evil was inside or outside of me. In the small hours of the morning, I sometimes took scissors and either sawed or snipped flaps of skin from the top of my thighs, high enough so that when I put on my shorts for PE class, the cuts wouldn't show. If they were deep enough to draw blood, I covered them with Band-Aids.

As the weeks went by, I missed more and more school. If a girl at my lunch table or a teacher asked why I was out sick so often, I gave them a line I'd come up with: I told them I had "a low tolerance for pain." That self-diagnosis was a way to explain why I hurt all the time, even though it seemed I was living the same life as every other thirteen-year-old girl I knew. The more days of school I missed, the more I fell behind, and the harder it was to go back.

My only incentive for going to class at all was that if I went, my parents allowed me to go online in the evenings. I'd sign into AOL and compose e-mails addressed to no one, choosing different background colors and font sizes for the perfect suicide note. From the library I'd checked out Sylvia Plath's journals, *An Actor Prepares* by Stanislavski (I was playing Violet in our drama club's production of *Charlie and the Chocolate Factory*), and the London cast recording of *Les Misérables*. I spent one Saturday afternoon listening to "On My Own" on repeat for seven hours, trying to decide which lyrics to quote in my suicide e-mail to Daniel.

It was May 1998. As my depression worsened, my suicide plan crystallized. My plan was my anchor in the storm. Thinking about how I would do it made me feel calm and in control, even smug; without anyone's help (not that anyone was offering any), I'd figured out the solution to my own problem.

I wanted to say good-bye to Daniel because he was the person I talked to more than anyone, my closest friend. Instead of just sending an e-mail, I told him over IM that on Thursday I was going to stay home from school and take all the prescription medication I'd collected around the house and saved in a Ziploc bag. Though I didn't know what any of the medication was for, I didn't think it mattered. He tried to talk me out of it, but I would not be dissuaded. I didn't want to be talked out of it. I just wanted to say good-bye. I had already been to the *If you are thinking of suicide, read this first* website more than once, and it had lost its persuasive effect.

But because there were no digital cameras, no Facebook profiles, because he'd had to mail that photograph of himself in a real envelope, Daniel knew my home address.

He called the police in my town.

The police called my school.

My school called my parents.

It was a real telephone tree. When my mom called me downstairs from my bedroom to tell me what she knew, I was furious at Daniel, and embarrassed that I would have to someday speak to him again, after all that time I'd spent planning the perfect good-bye. But I looked forward to what I thought would happen next: hospitalization.

I've spent almost two decades trying to understand what happened to my brain in a dark flash that spring, and so often I come back to the weather. You might think that suicides happen during fall and winter, when there's less sunlight and more people suffering from seasonal depression. But researchers have found that suicides peak around June in the northern hemisphere and December in the southern. In other words, suicide weather is warm and sunny.

At the turn of the twentieth century, a professor named Edwin G. Dexter gathered data from five years of New York City coroner's reports (twenty-eight thousand death certificates), found 1,962 suicides, and calculated the number of suicides for each of the 1,862 days of those years. Then he looked at police records to find out how many *unsuccessful* attempts there were, noting that "this record is quite complete, since in the eyes of the law one attempting suicide is a criminal, and must be so branded on the books." The total number of New Yorkers whose wish to die was recorded during those five years: 2,946.

Next, Dexter looked at meteorological records and correlated suicide occurrence with factors such as temperature, humidity, "character of day" (cloudy or clear), precipitation, and windiness. His findings showed the most attempts (successful and unsuccessful) occurring in April, May, and August, and concluded that "suicide is excessive under those conditions of weather which are generally considered most exhilarating and delightful— that is, the later spring months and upon clear, dry days."

The day before Emma Bovary's suicide is "one of those March days, clear and sharp, when the sun shines in a perfectly white sky."

Virginia Woolf filled her coat pockets with stones and walked into a nearby river on March 28, 1941. Her body was finally found on April 18.

A lot of famous people choose April, or April chooses them: Kurt Cobain, Hart Crane, Primo Levi, Vladimir Mayakovsky, Eva Braun. It took Eva three times to get it right (cyanide). The first (August 1932, pistol shot to the jugular) and second (May 1935, sleeping pill overdose) attempts were not fatal. Her biographer Angela Lambert writes that Eva's suicide attempts were motivated by a wish for Hitler to pay more attention to her; paradoxically, she had to be serious in their execution, but also manage to survive, or else she would miss the resulting attention.

"Hard to believe that Hitler might not have been a sensitive boyfriend," a friend joked when I told him about Eva's attempts.

August is for poets and actresses: Marilyn Monroe, Sylvia Plath (first attempt), Jean Seberg, Marina Tsvetaeva.

Why do I still keep this collection today—these names and dates and circumstances? Is it adolescent morbidity? Idolatry? Or am I playing at detective, collecting clues? Perhaps it was just pubescent hormones that scrambled my brain, or a genetic predisposition to depression made suddenly apparent at the age of thirteen, like a fairy-tale curse. Then I revisit the month of May and think maybe I was the victim of *clear, dry days, most exhilarating and delightful*. Charles Dudley Warner, a friend of Mark Twain's, famously quipped, "Everybody talks about the weather, but nobody does anything about it." Is it the poet in me who's so drawn to the idea of suicide weather, the paradox of the bright clear day that says *die*?

Sylvia Plath's successful second attempt was in February 1963. The doctor treating her in London couldn't get a bed for her at the hospital, and on February 4, he prescribed the antidepressant tranylcypromine, while they waited for space to become available. On February 10, Sylvia left bread and milk for her two sleeping children and then laid her head on a cloth inside the oven with the gas turned on. She was thirty years old. Her mother and her estranged husband, the poet Ted Hughes, both would blame the tranylcypromine for her death, arguing that her American doctors would have known she was allergic to it, and that the drug must have embellished the suicidal thoughts it was supposed to wipe away.

The hard truth: easier to blame a drug than to blame yourself for not doing more to save a life. My own hard truth: easier to collect my weather data than to tell you I was a ghost in my own house, suffering invisibly through the night while my therapist mother slept in the next room. Harder still: I idolized Sylvia because she gave me the words for my experience, but I've come to realize I was more like Eva Braun, wanting to be taken seriously, yet also survive.

As a young woman, my grandmother heard voices coming from the toilet and was misdiagnosed as schizophrenic. The voices were more likely symptomatic of her first manic episode; eventually, the doctors got it right and put her on lithium. My mom, having spent her adolescence helping to care for her three younger siblings while her mother was in and out of hospitals, went on to get her PhD in clinical psychology. The one time I told her about my voices as a child, she said I must have a fever and sent me to my room.

From the age of fifty onward, my grandmother lived in a nursing home, except when she became psychotic and they transferred her to the hospital. The antipsychotic drugs she'd been prescribed (to treat the schizophrenia she never had) had led her to develop tardive dyskinesia, a movement disorder that made her twitch, noticeably and uncontrollably, for the rest of her life. It was almost impossible to understand anything she said when she spoke.

By the time I was thirteen, I had also visited my paternal grandfather in the psychiatric ward, after he got laid off from a long career with Cadillac, and had a nervous breakdown.

On my visits to these hospitals, I saw what happens when you become too sick to care for yourself: your family brings you milk shakes; they pat you on the hand; they give you their undivided attention and don't ask for anything in return.

But my mom refused to have me hospitalized because she thought it would be more traumatic than therapeutic at my age. I took this as a sign that I hadn't tried hard enough. If I'd *really* attempted, then I'd already be admitted, in my nightgown. The only person who treated me like I was as sick as I felt was Daniel, who knew me only as a faceless voice.

On a Saturday morning, while my mom was seeing her own patients, my dad took me to my first psychiatrist appointment. My five-year-old sister, Hattie, was with us.

The waiting room was gray, sterile, nondescript. A fish tank stood against one wall, and the soft sucking sound of the water filter was the only noise in the room. I knew that seeing a therapist was a private thing to do, because sometimes my mom treated patients in her basement office at our house and I had to stay out of the way, unseen and quiet. Patients even used a separate entrance. But when it was my turn to see the psychiatrist, he brought us all into his office.

The doctor, a big man, was wedged into a leather armchair across from my seat on the couch. With his beard and huge, square-framed glasses, he instantly reminded me of my sixth-grade teacher, Mr. Grumbles (not a nickname), who always had food stuck in his beard after lunch.

Did he expect me to reveal all the reasons I wanted to die in front of my dad and sister? They were on the floor at my feet, quietly reading picture books, and playing with blocks. I thought maybe we could pretend that, like the audience of a play, they weren't there.

But the psychiatrist didn't even look at me. He asked my dad how I'd been sleeping.

My dad turned to me. "He wants to know how you've been sleeping," he said.

"A lot," I said.

"She says she's been sleeping a lot," he told the doctor.

"How much is a lot?"

"He says how much have you been sleeping," my dad translated.

"Eleven or twelve or thirteen hours."

"And how's her appetite?"

"I'm not hungry."

"She says she's not hungry."

"Any thoughts of suicide?"

Seriously? My dad just looked at me. He didn't repeat the question.

"*Yes*," I hissed. I wasn't being treated like I was crazy; I was being treated like a child, like I didn't speak the language of adults, but of course I understood each of his questions perfectly well: I'd taken depression symptom questionnaires online. I already had my answers prepared.

He prescribed Paxil, and recommended a woman I could see for talk therapy. My dad thanked him. His politeness was a betrayal.

Cecilia Lisbon, the youngest of the five sisters who die in the novel *The Virgin Suicides*, makes her first attempt in June, "slitting her wrists like a Stoic while taking a bath." After reviving her, the doctor in the ER asks what she's doing there. "You're not even old enough to know how bad life gets," he tells her.

"Obviously, Doctor," Cecilia says, "you've never been a thirteen-year-old girl." The perfect comeback—so self-aware, so pointed. How I wish I could have said something just like that to my psychiatrist, but depression slayed my wit, my gumption. Only a novelist could have invented that line for Cecilia.

The Paxil made me shake uncontrollably. In school or at play rehearsal, I had to sit on my hands. My teeth chattered. I kept my mouth shut. I was told the side effects would eventually go away, but how could I believe anything the adults said?

Part of my desperation to be hospitalized was so that I wouldn't have to finish out the school year. Since Daniel had called the police, I was no longer allowed to just stay home all day by myself. I was on "suicide watch." One morning, my parents had to peel my fingers from the bars of the bunk bed I shared with my sister and carry me, kicking and screaming, out to the minivan to drive me to school. I refused to go to class. As a compromise, I was allowed to sit in the guidance counselor's office and cry all day. On the wall of the counselor's office was a big poster that read I CAN ONLY PLEASE ONE PERSON PER DAY. TODAY IS NOT YOUR DAY. TOMORROW IS NOT LOOKING SO GOOD EITHER.

One of the few teachers I actually liked found me in the office that morning and looked surprised to find me crying. "Are you okay?" she asked.

I nodded. Which was a lie. But I didn't know what to say. Had no one told my teachers I wanted to kill myself? She hovered in the doorway for a second and then left me alone again with that fucking poster to stare at.

I missed so many days of seventh grade that I almost didn't pass on to eighth. Once my medication stabilized a little, I was assigned an aide, to help me finish all the schoolwork I was behind on. We worked in a room with floor-to-ceiling windows that faced the cafeteria. Any of my classmates who noticed my absence in Algebra could now watch me in this little room, like a panther behind bars, trying to solve problems that had once come easily to me and were now hopelessly unreachable through the fog in my head.

At our first meeting together, the woman looked me in the eye and, with a kindness that was uncharacteristic for employees of that school, told me gently that she knew how I felt: her daughter had struggled with depression, too.

I nodded politely. *That means you have no idea how I feel*, I thought.

Years later as an adult, I directed a production of *Charlie and the Chocolate Factory* with kids at a summer day camp in Coney Island. On the phone with my mom, I mentioned the costume she'd made for me when I played Violet.

"When you played Violet?"

"In seventh grade, remember?"

No, she didn't remember.

"I had that lavender gingham dress from Gap Kids . . . and you made two little loops out of elastic, so that when I put my wrists through them I could make the dress balloon out like a blueberry."

"That was such a horrible time," she finally said. "I feel so bad that I can't remember. There's so much I've blocked out."

I wished she could give me the gift that Jason gave so effortlessly: the words *of course I remember*. The gift of a witness.

❧

One night while I was waiting tables in Albuquerque, I served a family of four from out of town. They were all very warm and outgoing. When the dad asked what I was doing in Albuquerque, I said I used to teach the performing arts to kids, but now I was writing a book.

"About New Mexico?"

A lot of people assumed this. "No," I said, "it's about a baby-sitter."

"Oh. Well, I work with kids, too. I'm the director of a children's theater company in Las Vegas."

I only knew one person in Las Vegas, and he was a member of a children's theater company. I gave him Daniel's name.

"Of course I know Daniel!" he said. "How do you know him?"

"We met online when we were thirteen," I said, "on an Andrew Lloyd Webber fan club message board."

He laughed. "That's incredible," he said.

After work I found Daniel on Facebook and friended him.

The Gaslight Diner
(2007)

During that Albuquerque fall, I started taking the Zoloft and the Ativan. Taking an Ativan turned the volume down. Jason could yell at me, he could give me the long explanations for why he'd lost this job (movie studio security guard) or that one (Olive Garden waiter), he could leave me and go ride somewhere, and I wouldn't care. It turned off the part of me that cared.

But I·was still depressed. And running out of pills.

"There's no psychiatrist who will see me for *months*," I complained to my mom, over the phone.

"You're not in Chicago anymore," she said.

Clearly.

She tracked down Dr. Schultz, my psychiatrist from middle and high school, and made a phone appointment for me. He was the third doctor I saw in adolescence, after the initial Mr. Grumbles look-alike, and then a woman who told me, when I said I thought I was getting better, that she didn't think I was qualified to make that assessment. Dr. Schultz never spoke to me like someone who wasn't qualified to make her own assessments. Whenever we talked about teenage girl body issues, he acknowledged how difficult it must be to grow up in the body of a young woman, without presuming that he knew what it felt like to *be* a young woman. We also talked a lot about acting and identity. Most important, he spoke to me like I was intelligent, even though I worried that I no longer was. Depression had killed my powers of concentration, my creativity, and my curiosity—traits I'd never thought to cherish as a child because how could I have known they'd go away?

Dr. Schultz was the one who'd cured me of my voices as a teenager. "Have you ever asked them to go away and leave you alone?" he asked.

I'd shaken my head. "I never thought of that," I admitted. I'd always felt like their victim, powerless, but the next time they came, I tried it. I told them to go away and they did. I haven't heard them in over ten years.

Before our call, I Googled the doctor and found on his website that he specialized in treating adolescent ADHD, which had nothing to do with me, since I was an adult—at least I felt like I was an adult. Wanted to be an adult. But I was still so dependent. Everyone wanted to help me, but no one could. No doctor's appointment, no book, no medication, no late-night intervention was going to keep me away from Jason, as much as I sometimes wished for a rescue. It was hard to get anyone to understand my conflicting desires: I wanted to be protected from Jason while also staying with him. Imagine if Rapunzel got saved from her tower but then the prince let her visit the witch on the weekends, for that familiar pain, that yank of the hair—that's what I wanted.

I didn't say any of this to Dr. Schultz. I'd always felt comfortable telling him anything, whether about hearing voices or cutting myself, and here was my opportunity to speak candidly about my life with Jason. But I had to be realistic about where I was, and what I could hope to get from our single phone call.

"I live in New Mexico now, with my boyfriend," I said, getting straight to the point. "He told me I have to be on medication because I'm too crazy without it. He thinks I have trichotillomania, too."

"Why does he think that?"

"Because I pluck my eyebrows twice a day."

Dr. Schultz chuckled. "You know," he said, "my niece was staying with us over the weekend, and she brought so many . . . accessories with her, hair straighteners and all that, it was just amazing. I can't imagine having to be a young woman today."

"So . . . you don't think I have trichotillomania?"

"You can tell your boyfriend that your doctor says you do not have trichotillomania."

I felt like I'd scored a point against Jason.

I told him about my anxiety attacks, and about seeing a general practitioner who would give me only ten Ativans. "Wow," Dr. Schultz said. "Very conservative." He said he would call in a prescription for Wellbutrin to add to the Zoloft, and thirty Ativans.

At least I had my pharmaceutical cure. No one was coming to save me, but I hoped the pills would make my life in the tower easier to endure.

The new medication knocked me out, turned the volume even lower. My metabolism went through the roof, and I always felt on the verge of fainting, like a Victorian heroine. I tried to regulate my life with a routine that was independent of Jason's chaos: make breakfast, take pills, write, eat lunch, check the mail, go to work, eat protein bars to stay upright, come home, eat dinner, stare at the wall. According to Jason, this wasn't any better than the way I'd been before. He would call my mom because "she's a professional and it's her job to help us." One night I overheard him tell her that I would always be sick, that she would be caring for her sick daughter forever.

I didn't see it then, but I see it now: although my voices went away as a teenager, in Jason I found their qualified replacement. The sicker he said I was, the more it seemed to be true: I was the victim of something beyond my control, and I would be its victim forever, always dependent on others to help me live my life. To disprove this theory I would have had to leave him and forge ahead on my own. I couldn't do that. He made me believe the story he told me about myself, and I stayed with him because if he was right then it meant he was the only one who truly saw me.

At the diner, the girls were me, Ruth, Jenna, KJ, Anna, Lois, Claudette, and Stephanie. KJ was the oldest, a mother of five, and she wore special shoes for her bad back. Stephanie was the most beautiful and also the quietest. Claudette once made pot brownies and Ruth got so high off one that she had to leave work and go home. Jenna was always stoned, her pupils like dark moons when I said hi to her near the salad prep station. Lois was homeless, living in a halfway house. Anna went to school.

We were white and Hispanic and Navajo. On the books we made $2.17 an hour. In the computer every night we had to enter 10 percent of our sales, whether we made that much in tips or not. To legally serve alcohol in the state of New Mexico, I had to take a daylong class taught by a grad student in American history, in which we watched videos of drunk driving accidents and pledged to serve greasy food like fries to sober any customer who seemed too sauced. On the diner menu, you could choose from three different kinds of wine: red, white, or pink. We poured it from a spigot in a box.

When Stephanie rolled up the cuffs of her T-shirt I could see the bruises her boyfriend's hands had left on her arms in the shape of a grip. We all worried about her but felt there was nothing we could do for her other than avoid talking about the bruises because she didn't want to talk about them. Luis, who worked in the kitchen, was in love with Stephanie. He was on probation, but I couldn't imagine what his crime had been because he was so gentle and funny and warm. In his spare time, he did custom paint jobs on cars. When Stephanie came in busted, or didn't show up for her shift, Luis's face would pale and he'd swear to us that he was going to kill her boyfriend. On those days, we didn't joke around with him when picking up our orders from the heated window.

Mike and Matthew were the teenage busboys who made me coffee malts and drove me home at night after my shift if Jason couldn't or wouldn't come and get me. Mike snorted coke, which made us worry about him, but Matthew just smoked pot all the time, which seemed okay—therapeutic even—because his dad had just died.

There were coin-operated jukeboxes at each of the tables in the diner, and Jess, the nineteen-year-old cashier, kept an emergency stash of quarters to save us from Patsy Cline's "I Fall to Pieces" coming on again. Since about 50 percent of the staff was high at any given time, we'd always rather hear "Splish Splash" or "Purple People Eater."

During the busy season around the holidays, Warren, one of the managers, hired someone new to alternate shifts with Jess at the register. Misty was older, probably late thirties, and wore high-waisted jeans with her standard-issue Route 66 T-shirt tucked in. Almost everything about her was big—she was tall with big boobs, big hips, big legs, big arms. But her voice was high and thin and always on the verge of cracking. Whether she was talking to me, or giving someone change for their bill, it sounded like she was going to cry. She was so awkward it made some of the other waitresses uncomfortable, and they badgered Warren about why he had hired her.

"Be nice," he said. "You don't know her whole story. She really needs this, and I said we'd try her out and see if it works."

I wanted to be nice to her. Not just because Warren said so, but because I was drawn to her weirdness, her vulnerability. At the diner, I got to meet all kinds of people who were nothing like me. More than once, Warren had had to pull me away from one of my tables because I'd been there for too long, asking my customers where they had come from and where they were going.

Near closing, when it finally slowed down in my section, I would go talk to Misty. She wore her coppery hair clipped back in a half ponytail, and her darker roots showed. I asked her about her life, where she was from, what she was doing now.

"I live with my boyfriend," she told me.

"Me, too," I said.

"He's younger."

"Mine, too!"

We bonded over this single commonality. Eventually she told me *younger* meant *teenage*. Misty was suspended from her job as a special ed teacher; that's why she'd needed new work. She was suspended because she was in a romantic relationship with her student. He was eighteen or nineteen, old enough that it wasn't illegal, just inappropriate and shocking. I listened and nodded. Who was I to judge? We had the same problems with our teen-age boyfriends, nagging them to keep up with their share of responsibilities when they just wanted to play video games. Some nights Misty gave me a ride home in her Jeep. How she'd met her boyfriend wasn't even her most surprising story; one night, rat-tled, she told me she'd just seen her sister, who admitted she was in an incestuous relationship with their father. "She rubbed it in my face," Misty said. "We didn't see him for years, but still. What am I supposed to say?"

It would be easy to say that I gawked at Stephanie's bruises and listened to Misty's stories because they made my own life seem better by contrast. I admit that, like a tourist to a disaster site, I witnessed the misery of my coworkers. I had chosen Albuquerque as my destination and I could leave when and if I wanted to: this was my privilege. But at the time, I didn't think of my life with

Jason as a story worth telling. I had no perspective on what was happening to me. I listened to Misty, and nodded sympathetically, and patted her shoulder when her eyes filled with tears, because I saw that it helped. It was the only thing I could do for her.

It took a long time for Lois to tell me she was homeless. She was a recovering alcoholic who had escaped an abusive husband. Lois was blonde and had the skin of someone who had grown up in the sun. She seemed hard and soft at the same time. When Jason unexpectedly showed up at the diner one night to tell me he'd spoken to my mom on the phone and told her about all the pot I smoked and how he believed it was making me psychotic, it was Lois who took the coffeepot out of my hands, steered me by my shoulders to the back parking lot, where we bleached the cutting boards each night, and calmed me by the light of the moon.

Four nights a week I waited tables and one night a week I took the number sixty-six bus to my friend Ellen's apartment near UNM, for our writing workshop. Ellen was about fifteen years older than me, with dark curly hair, a dry sense of humor, and a kind of rare laugh that had to be truly earned. I found out about Ellen and her writing group online, and even when other members dropped out, Ellen and I continued to meet on a weekly basis. More than anyone, she supported the reason Jason and I had supposedly moved to Albuquerque in the first place: the novel I was writing.

"Don't shoot yourself," begins one of Ellen's critiques, "but I haven't pulled any punches because I want you to sell your book." She was tough on me not because there was something wrong with me or my writing, but because she took my work and my potential seriously. I was used to going after what I wanted like a wild horse, ready to buck anyone who stood in my way, but Ellen trained and contained me, showed me how much I still had to learn and practice.

Here was someone I could have told about what happened in the six days between each of our meetings. I could have asked her what she thought I should do if the young man I loved was diligently working to persuade me that anything that was wrong with our relationship was caused by my mood disorder. But as much as I yearned for some reasonable person to tell me I didn't have to live like this, I also didn't want to be the young naïve waitress with relationship drama. That was one part of my life; Ellen's book-filled apartment was a refuge from the turmoil.

I never told her anything.

The Proposal

(2007–11)

A couple of months before Jason and I moved to Albuquerque, when we were still living in suburban Chicagoland, we went to a Memorial Day weekend party he'd heard about through a friend of a friend. At one in the morning, we knocked on the door and a giddy blonde girl answered and told us she'd been doing Jägerbombs with her mom, who was now passed out upstairs. Then she walked away. Thanks to the sleepovers of my childhood, this house was the kind of suburban split-level ranch I knew how to navigate without ever having been there before. We walked through the dining room and kitchen and let ourselves out onto the concrete patio in the back. The night was humid, heavy with the hum of air-conditioning units. Jason took a shot and opened a beer. I stood by, sober. Before the party, we'd gotten into a fight and I'd tried to break up with him; he'd suggested I stop drinking because it made me too emotional.

Within a few minutes of our arrival, the doorbell rang. A gangly boy peeked over the privacy fence and saw cop cars parked out front. Everyone at the party was underage, except for me, and, presumably, the girl's mom. There was knocking on the door. There was nowhere to run. The fence was too high. The blonde became hysterical and said we should all hide in her basement.

"And you think that will make them go away?" Jason swallowed the last of his beer and said he would answer the door. The more the blonde begged him not to, the more revved up he got.

I followed the two of them into the house and then stood off to the side, as Jason opened the door for the two police officers standing on the front porch.

"This your party?"

"No, sir," Jason said, and pointed at the girl.

"Are your parents home?"

"No," she said gravely.

"Better call them, then," the cop said.

For the next two hours, everyone had to take a Breathalyzer and decide whether to call their parents and tell them what had happened, or spend the night in jail. A teenage boy and I were the only sober ones; we sat at the dining room table quietly while everyone else took the test and called their parents. The blonde kept her cell phone to her ear and insisted that her mom wasn't home. No, she didn't know when she'd be back (we'd find out later that her mom was coaching her by phone from the bedroom to say she wasn't home, so she wouldn't be arrested for serving alcohol to kids). I wasn't allowed to get up from the table and go talk to Jason, who was waiting in line to be Breathalyzed, but I knew he wouldn't want to call his dad and I didn't want him to sleep in jail. So when it came time for his turn, I stood up and asked if they'd let me take him home, since I was twenty-two, sober, and we were living together (loosely defined by my sleeping over at Jason's one-bedroom apartment every night since I'd "won" him from Veronika).

"I'll take responsibility for him," I said.

"What are you," the cop sneered, "his mom or his girlfriend? If you were his wife, I might say yes."

I felt belittled and frustrated, but before I could think of anything feisty to say in return Jason dropped to one knee. He took off the ring he always wore, a plain band soldered from a motorcycle part, and asked if I would marry him. I laughed and said yes. He put the ring on my finger. Both cops gave a slow clap. I touched the ring, felt how warm the band was from being close to his skin. I spun it in a loop around my finger. I knew I would have to give it back, but I wouldn't have wanted to keep it anyway. The ring had been a gift from his first girlfriend's dad, a motorcycle mechanic, who'd made them a matching set. It was too big for any of my fingers.

"Sorry," one of the cops said, "but we're still going to have to take you in," and made Jason turn around while he put the handcuffs on. Jason was all *yes, sir, no, sir.* I was all out of ideas. They hadn't put the cuffs on anyone else, but all the other kids had called their parents.

At last, after all the kids were sobered and gone, they let Jason go. The whole thing had been a show, for a scare. They said we could go and we had to say thank you. I still had the ring. In the car, I gave it back. We stayed up the rest of the night, driving, smoking, talking, replaying the scene, what everyone's faces had looked like, how brilliant we were, until it turned from night to day and McDonald's started serving breakfast.

This was the story I told his family, in his grandmother's living room, the night before his funeral. When I arrived at the part where he gets down on one knee, everyone laughed. They could picture the scene. For a brief moment, I'd brought him back to life.

Then his mom passed around a Ziploc bag of the things found on his body at the scene of the accident. A wallet with a single dollar in it. A mini flashlight. The same ring from that night. I almost couldn't believe I was holding it again; the only time I ever saw him take it off was when he proposed. I was shocked that they weren't going to bury him wearing it, but couldn't think of a polite way to say, *You give that back*. How could I say this to his mother, whom I'd only just met?

I made eyes at his ex-girlfriend Lisa, whom he had dated for years after we broke up, and we went to sit in the corner together, conspiratorially, like girls at a dance. Lisa was petite and funny and charismatic, someone I'd become fast friends with if only I had met her under other circumstances. "Don't you think he should be buried with the ring?" I whispered.

She nodded. Then she said, "But you know he wouldn't have wanted to be buried at all. Jason told me he wanted to be cremated."

I didn't remember him ever telling me this, but it was also possible that he did and I just forgot. I liked Lisa (I *wanted* to like her) but I was not ready to admit she might know anything about Jason that I did not. And what if she was wrong? Not wrong, but misremembering?

"You're right," I told her. "I'd forgotten that, but he told me, too."

Then I excused myself and went to the kitchen to make myself a taco plate. Not only was I the only one who seemed hungry, but my hunger was embarrassingly insatiable. Food fast-forwarded time for me: first tacos, then bed, then the funeral, then I would fly home. I was scooping seconds onto my plate when Jason's grandmother and I started talking about his recent obsession with diet and exercise. I told her I remembered all the vitamins he took from a gallon-sized Ziploc bag when he stayed with me in Brooklyn. The last e-mail Jason ever sent me was about research he'd been doing on how antioxidant supplements could combat the daily accumulation of free radicals and prolong life. The last line of the e-mail: *Immortality ahoy? I'll let you be the judge.*

"I still have one of his fruit smoothies in the fridge," she said.

The fridge was right behind her.

My first thought was, *Can I see it?*

My second thought was, *Why do I want to see it?*

Because his mouth was on that straw, that's why I wanted to see it. And because his finger was wearing that ring until they removed it from his body. Because when I think of Jason the first thing I always think of is his body. That night, for the last time, his body lay aboveground. I could easily imagine him rising from his coffin and coming for us, demanding we return the ring before he'd go anywhere. I thought, *He'll never let us live this down.*

Dawn Patrol

(2007)

In Albuquerque, Rick and Vicky lived in the apartment across from ours with their two daughters, Scarlet and Tana—these were the girls I'd seen thrown in the air at the pool on the day before I flew back to Chicago. They were our neighbors and, for a few months, our friends. One night after the girls were in bed, Vicky and I dispatched the guys to Blockbuster to rent *Death Proof* and popped fresh cans of Coors Light. Alone together for the first time, we quickly spilled the stories of how we'd gotten to where we were, our shortcut to the kind of intimacy between friends who've actually lived through each other's lives. Vicky told me she was originally from Milwaukee, and had ended up in Albuquerque via Baltimore, because of a government job testing anthrax on monkeys.

"What about you? Did you guys move here for a job?"

"Well, Jason said he would work while I wrote a book."

"About New Mexico?"

"No," I said. "It's about a guy who has an affair with his daughter's babysitter."

Vicky had a tough, scratchy laugh. She looked a little like Toni Collette, but with a spotty complexion. "Just ask my husband," she said, and then got up for another beer before I could ask a follow-up question. Rick, her husband, had once been a plumber, but now he stayed at home and watched the girls while Vicky worked. He hid his baldness under caps.

One afternoon Jason went to fly kites with Rick and the girls in the park across the street, and came back to report that Rick carried a Big Gulp cup filled with whiskey and ice with him at all times.

Whenever I had the night off from waitressing we'd go over to their place, drink beer, and watch *Rock of Love with Bret Michaels* on VH1 (Vicky was Team Heather; I was for Jes), while Scarlet and Tana played dress up in scarves and necklaces and sat in our laps, begging me and Jason to save them from bedtime. When we were all on the couch it was hard to tell, but Vicky was taller than Rick.

Just ask my husband—I couldn't get this line out of my head. Each weekday morning, as I sat writing at my desk, I watched the same young blonde woman cross the parking lot and go inside their apartment. She wore a rotation of velour tracksuits. Her face was very pretty and symmetrical, like a reality show contestant's, but I never saw her smile. I never saw her without a cigarette either. She looked so lethargic I thought she had to be on drugs. In the afternoons, she'd be back outside, making slow laps around the parking lot with a blond boy I assumed was her son, who looked about twelve, and who rode his bike without paying any attention to the cars coming in and out.

"Well, it's obvious what's going on," Jason said, when I told him about my spying.

"What's obvious, that they're having an affair? But Rick is home with the girls all day."

"I'm going to ask him if he's sleeping with her."

"Oh my God, don't."

"I'm going to," he said.

I tried to be optimistic: maybe Rick and Vicky had some kind of arrangement. A couple of weekends in a row, I'd seen her around our apartment complex with another man. He was tall, nice-looking. Unlike Rick, he wore his shirt tucked into his jeans. Scarlet and Tana and Vicky all took turns holding his hands.

The next time I was alone with Vicky I asked her about the blonde woman.

"Oh, that's just the girls' babysitter's daughter," she said. I tried to understand why they had a babysitter to begin with, if Rick stayed at home, not to mention why her daughter would be at their apartment for half of each day.

And the other man?

"He's a friend from work," she said. I got the sense that it would be rude to press. It was none of my business.

"Now can I ask you a question?"

"Sure," I said.

"Do you come from money?"

Her question stung—after working with kids for twelve hours a day all summer to save money for our move, I was now waiting tables and dipping into my savings to make sure our rent and utilities were covered each month. And between moving expenses and our security deposit and my plane ticket home to Chicago, my savings were almost completely depleted. Far from "supporting" us, Jason's paychecks always seemed to spend themselves—on gas and cigarettes, fast food and weed. He was like my teenage son. In fact, he was a teenager, but I needed him to grow up faster. Jason had recently quit his maintenance job because he said it was too physically exhausting, and it was a couple of weeks before he got a new job, canvassing for the environment, which meant standing outside all day and flirting with women until they donated money.

"No," I told Vicky. "We moved here with my savings and now we're both working."

Only years later would I understand the subtext of her question. Vicky saw that the decisions that had landed us in the city where she lived had been made on a whim. She recognized that Jason and I had enough support, somehow, somewhere, to make big leaps without thinking too much about the consequences. But at the time, I didn't feel like I had any support. In Albuquerque I so often felt like the sole party responsible, the only adult in the room.

A few days after my conversation with Vicky, Rick knocked on our door and asked Jason if he could borrow twenty bucks. Jason didn't have it either. He asked me.

"Why does he need money?" I hissed.

"He says to buy a carton of cigarettes. He'll pay you back."

I found it inconceivable that he didn't have twenty dollars, and that he would come over and ask me for it. Did Vicky think I was lying about where my money came from? All my waitressing tips were on my desk, in a purse shaped like a Chinese takeout container. Jason knew that's where I kept them, and even that made me uncomfortable. I didn't want to open my purse in front of Rick.

While I was deliberating over what to do, Jason seized the opportunity. "Can I ask you a question?"

"Shoot," Rick said.

"It's kind of personal. Maybe we should go in the other room."

"Jason," I warned. "Don't."

"I'm not going in the other room with you, man."

"I'll go in the other room, then." I started moving toward the bedroom.

"No, I want you to hear this," Jason said. "There's this blonde woman we see walking around the parking lot—"

"Crystal?"

"Is that her name, Crystal? Are you sleeping with her?"

Rick was standing in our kitchen. He looked cold, furious. "Even if I were," he said, "it would be none of your business."

I told Rick I was sorry, but I didn't have any cash I could lend him, and he left.

⚜

Autumn in Albuquerque was bright sun and crisp air, chile ristras hanging to dry from all the eaves. For days leading up to the international hot air balloon fiesta in October, every time Jason said *fiesta*, I replied, "*¡Olé!*" We stayed up all night so that we could arrive at the park before sunrise, grabbing breakfast burritos and hot chocolates and then finding a spot to sit in the damp dawn grass. Our breath blew clouds in the cold. Across the dark field, the balloons weren't yet lit.

"Someday I'm going to marry you," Jason said.

"What do you mean 'someday'?"

"I mean I'm young now, and I have to go and have other experiences. But just you wait."

Actually, I didn't want to wait. It wasn't that I wanted to get married to him immediately, but I wanted to know how our story would end. I felt acute panic at the idea of him having "other experiences" without me, at the thought of being left behind. With Jason, I felt like I was standing under stage lights—it was too hot, maybe even uncomfortable, but everyone sitting in the dark could see me. With him, I was a bright young thing. And when I forced myself to imagine life without him, he got to stay onstage but I had to go back and sit in the shadows and watch.

One by one, the balloons were ignited and the Dawn Patrol began. It was beautiful to witness the launch of these huge, glowing bulbs. Close to us, on the ground, the balloons appeared as big as houses, but as they rose into the sky they grew smaller and smaller until they were just resplendent thumbprints. With my disposable camera, I took a picture of Jason, wearing his Ray-Bans, fingers pointed. Behind him the sky was a corona of blue.

A week before Thanksgiving, Jason woke me in the middle of the night.

"What's wrong?" I said.

"Vicky is here. She says she wants to talk to you."

I found her standing in our living room in a Looney Tunes sweatshirt and a pair of socks, hugging herself, crying and wiping her nose on her sleeve. Drunk. It was Rick's fortieth birthday, she said. She'd started an argument about getting a divorce, the fight had escalated, and Rick had taken the batteries out of her phone so she couldn't call the police.

"Then I kicked him in the balls and he started hitting my legs with his fists like this," she said, violently demonstrating.

"I'm calling the police," Jason said.

"No, don't," Vicky said. "I'm so humiliated. Please don't."

"Why do you let him treat you like this?" he said. "You deserve better than him. He's an asshole. You need to leave him. You should take Scarlet and Tana and go to a shelter." He lit a cigarette and paced around the kitchen with a cause to fight for. I rubbed Vicky's thin back.

"Can I bum a cigarette?"

"Sure," he said, and handed her the pack.

"I have to work in the morning. This is so humiliating."

I felt humiliated for her. Her cheeks were flush with gin blossoms, her eyes swollen from crying. I didn't know what to do. The phrase *domestic violence* popped into my head and hung there, like a banner above a carnival scene. If she had come over when I was home alone and begged me not to call the police, I never would have. But I wasn't home alone. Jason was there, and he called 911 to report a domestic dispute. After enduring an adolescence locked up in treatment centers and wilderness reform programs, Jason was galvanized by any opportunity to be on the offensive. Rick's behavior gave Jason the opportunity to play the hero.

While we waited for the cops to arrive, Vicky pulled herself together. She went in the bathroom and splashed water on her face, lit a fresh cigarette, prepared for her performance. First we saw the siren lights through the patio doors, and then I watched through the peephole as the cops walked over to Rick and Vicky's. I opened our door. "Over here," I whispered. They turned around.

"This isn't the first time we've been here, is it?" the female cop asked. Vicky said nothing. When prompted, she told them the same story she told us, except when they hinted at arresting her husband, Vicky changed her mind and said forget it, she'd sign whatever they wanted her to sign as long as she could go home.

"Isn't there a shelter she can go to?" Jason asked.

Vicky glared at him.

"I can give you a list of shelters," the female cop said.

"I'm not going to a shelter."

Her partner chimed in. "You are not allowed to sleep at home tonight, ma'am. Do you understand that?"

"I just want to go home."

"She can stay on our couch," I said, trying to appease everyone. This was the second time in my life I'd interacted with the police; the first had been the night of the proposal.

Finally the police left, after Vicky signed a report and accepted a photocopied list of battered women shelters, and then she asked us what we'd do if she went home anyway.

Jason said he'd call the police again.

"You're a real asshole, you know that?"

While Jason was in the bathroom, she asked me if I thought he meant what he said. I nodded, scared for both of us. There was no one, nothing, that would keep Jason from doing what he wanted to do. I could only try and think of things to say while she smoked the time away, waiting for Jason to change his mind and let her go.

"In a couple of days we're going to Las Vegas," I told her, "for his dad's wedding. I've never been there before."

Vicky looked me in the eye. She was sober now. "When you go to Vegas," she said, "don't get married."

"Don't worry, we won't," I said.

"I mean it," she said. "That's what Rick and I did. We thought it would be funny."

That night, she slept on the couch. I wanted to go back to bed, but Jason made me sleep with him on the floor near the front door to guard the exit. At five thirty the next morning, I loaned her a sports bra and a pair of shoes that she could wear to work. When I offered to let her use our shower, she said she always showered at work anyway, before dressing in the special chemical suit she wore while infecting monkeys with disease.

We drove to Las Vegas. By November, I knew how to drive stick, but Jason wanted to be behind the wheel for all 575 miles. Along I-40 W, I cranked the window down so I could stick out my arm and photograph the brambles and the life-sized dinosaur statues and teepee souvenir shops. We watched the landscape change from dusty flats to rusty mesas and back to dusty flats, beneath a sky colored like Renaissance paintings of heaven. In Nevada, we paused at the Hoover Dam and I made Jason pose with the river behind him.

Then, just outside Vegas, our tire blew. We made it to the

parking garage at our hotel, and Jason's dad, Victor, met us in his shiny rental car and took us to the rehearsal dinner. He had just bought a Garmin GPS, which he showed off to us; I'd never seen one before.

"Look, I can make her speak French," Victor said, changing a setting. "This would have been good to have when we were actually in France, huh?" he asked his fiancée, Maria. She was a pianist, twenty years his junior, and they traveled the world together so she could perform in competitions for emerging musicians. Maria was also the heiress to a small fortune from a chain of Midwestern fast-food restaurants, the number one reason (according to Jason) that Victor was marrying her. "He'll cheat on her, just watch," Jason had warned me. "He cheats on all of them."

At dinner, no one drank. Tucked away in an ornate private dining room at an Italian restaurant, the atmosphere felt more awkward than celebratory. It was a small wedding party— Victor's parents lived in Vegas and were too old to travel very often, which was why he had chosen this place for the ceremony. In addition to his mom and dad, his adopted sister came, plus two friends of his fiancée's and her parents. None of Victor's friends were there. No one tried to engage me or Jason in conversation. It seemed like they all saw us as children, and expected us to be quiet and well behaved in exchange for unlimited soft drinks.

"Leigh is writing a book," Jason, hyped up on Sprite, announced to the table.

"Oh, that's right," Maria said. "How's that going?"

"I've written almost ninety pages."

"And how long is a book supposed to be?" Victor asked.

"Two hundred and something."

Someone changed the subject, and Victor paid the check. He also paid for our room, at one of the crappier hotels on the strip, far from the hotel where he, Maria, and her friends were staying. It was too expensive, he said, to put us up there, too. I started to wonder if we should have even come at all—I'd thought Victor would want his only son at his wedding, but he seemed burdened by us. Had our invitation just been a formality? Had he been hoping we wouldn't be able to attend? I remembered a few months earlier, during the summer before we moved, when Victor and Maria first told us they were engaged. "Am I invited to the wedding?" Jason asked them. I thought he was joking. Jason idolized his dad, and the successful career he'd built as a logistics strategy consultant for multinational corporations, but Victor was always traveling or golfing or otherwise MIA. From Victor, Jason learned the power of keeping those who love you at arm's length.

The wedding was held the next day, in a chapel at one of the casinos. There was a small brunch reception after the ceremony in a cavernous ballroom. Jason made Maria's friends—two gay men—laugh, and they snuck him gin and tonics from the bartender. After the reception, we found a liquor store within walking distance and I got more gin we could drink back in our hotel room. We slept all afternoon and then stayed out all night. Jason convinced me that marijuana was legal in Vegas, so we smoked joints on the strip, collected postcards that advertised escorts, ate deep-fried Twinkies, rode the roller coaster through New York, New York, and got grilled cheese and fries at midnight. I won at blackjack and then lost all my winnings. We did not get married.

On our last day in Vegas, Victor took us to get our tire replaced. I stood in the sunny parking lot of the mechanic shop and watched them argue over whether Jason was sufficiently grateful for the secondhand car with a flat tire that we'd driven through two states because we couldn't afford to fly.

"This car was a gift to you. From Maria," Victor reminded him.

"Yeah," Jason said, "I know. It was her crappy car in college, and now she drives a BMW."

Victor pulled him aside so that Maria and I wouldn't hear what he said next. I stared at the palm trees in the distance. When they were finished talking, I awkwardly hugged Maria and Victor and said good-bye. I thanked him for everything, even though I privately wished we had either paid our share (of the dinner, the hotel, the flat tire) or not come to the wedding at all—I hated the way Victor felt he had to remind us we were in his debt. And Jason hated it even more than I did. Later, Jason would tell me that the reason Victor wanted a private conversation was in order to chastise him for not being nice to Maria, and then to threaten to stop communicating with him completely, if Jason didn't promise to like her.

With our new tire, we drove to the outskirts of Vegas to visit his grandparents before we went home. Their ranch house sat in the shade of a willow acacia tree. His grandfather was a locally famous poker player, and when we went to a casino buffet for lunch that day, everyone greeted him by name. Before Vegas, they'd lived in Albuquerque for years, so his grandmother and I talked about the sky and the Sandias. I told her about the balloon fiesta. I realized these were the first people we'd really talked to in days, the first people who wanted to talk about anything other than themselves.

"You're both welcome to come visit us anytime," his grandmother said, hugging me good-bye in the casino parking garage.

I never got a chance to tell Vicky we'd successfully avoided the wedding chapel. After the night she came over, we never spoke again. She left a plastic grocery bag with the sports bra and sneakers I'd lent her on my doormat. One night, Rick came into the diner for a beer, seemed surprised to see me working there, and told me what an asshole my boyfriend was and how I deserved better. His eyes were pinkish and out of focus. He hugged me good-bye and kissed my cheek. One of the busboys asked if there was a problem and I said it was okay, that he was my neighbor. Jason and I later found a notice to appear in court taped to their apartment door.

We were back from Vegas in time for Thanksgiving. I'd never cooked a turkey before, but I had my illustrated *Better Homes and Gardens* cookbook, and Jason said he knew how to make mashed potatoes. We bought a frozen turkey at Walmart (after I lost the argument that we should just buy turkey breasts), not realizing it needed twenty-four hours to thaw. I spent all day thawing it gradually in a couple of inches of cold water in the sink. When it was soft enough that I could reach inside to remove the neck and giblets, I burst into tears.

"It feels like a cold dead baby," I told him.

"Are you crying for real?"

At midnight, dinner was finally ready. Jason sawed at the turkey with a steak knife and we ate in silence in front of the TV. Though my parents had called earlier to wish me a happy

Thanksgiving, I realized that neither of Jason's parents had called him. Jason asked how I was going to be somebody's wife someday, if I didn't know how to cook a turkey.

For a long time I saw only two possible endings to our story: either Jason had to die or we had to get married. In my imagination, both endings seemed equally as likely, equally as horrifying. If we got married, I would lose my family's love and support and all my dreams for myself that didn't include him. If he died, I was sure I would lose the most exciting part of my life. Holding death and marriage in my hands like a scale of justice, I could never decide which would be better and which would be worse.

Pure Imagination

(2011)

The night before the funeral, after dinner at Jason's grandmother's house, his half brother T drove us to a bar in North Little Rock. We ordered round after round of whiskey shots. "To Jason!" we said each time, laughing, temporarily forgetting what we were toasting with such joie de vivre. A metal band was playing, and we all had to yell to be heard. I got drunk enough to ask Lisa if Jason ever hit her. "Oh yeah," she said, "but I hit him back. I scratched his eyes. I kicked him in the balls."

I had never thought of hitting him back.

"We threatened to call the cops on each other," she added.

I had never thought to do that either.

Over the music, Lisa yelled that sometimes, during their fights, she would beg him for his cell phone so that she could call me, because she knew who I was from his stories of New Mexico and imagined that I was someone who'd understand what was going on. His brother T joked that during these fights, Jason must have started to make the sound "Lee" and then followed it with a "Suh," once he remembered which girlfriend he was fighting with.

I stumbled out into the street to call Brian, back in New York. "I met Jason's ex-girlfriend Lisa, and she's just like *me*," I said, "but Korean! I wish we could be best friends!"

"Are you drunk?"

"I just wish I could, like, tell him that we met and how much I like her, you know?" I started to tear up, and said I'd have to call him back later.

For my twenty-third birthday, in Albuquerque, Jason used the candles to spell my name phonetically in the cake. Like the time he told me I didn't need surgery for ears that stick out too far, the candles said he loved me for who I was, but I didn't want to be who I was if there was always this risk of losing him to someone who was what I was not. Maybe that was why I felt so close to Lisa. She wasn't a dancer or a model. She was a PhD student in clinical psychology. She had big cheeks like mine, and a too-loud laugh.

Back inside the bar, I kept tucking the same piece of hair behind one ear, where it wouldn't stay. It wouldn't stay because it was too short. It was too short because when Jason visited me in Brooklyn, he fell asleep with gum in his mouth that got caught in my hair in the night. In the morning, he had asked me where my scissors were, and snipped off a four-inch chunk of my hair, before I could think of another solution. And then he was getting ready to leave for the airport. He was standing in my bedroom. I smoothed his blue T-shirt across his shoulders and kissed him on the mouth and said good-bye. I couldn't wait for him to go, to give me back my life in Brooklyn. I already knew I would not answer the phone the next time he called. It was the last time I ever spoke to him or saw him alive.

Lisa told me that the same thing happened to her. Before she even realized what he was doing, he'd gotten scissors and cut not only the strands stuck with gum, but almost all her dark hair.

His funeral would be the first she'd ever been to. She didn't know anyone else who had died.

The next morning at the funeral parlor, Victor fell on my shoulder, crying, when he saw me. He had his new girlfriend with him, the woman he'd cheated on his third wife, Maria, with. The new girlfriend had met Jason once. When Jason died, Victor hadn't spoken to his son in a year.

A TV mounted to the wall played a slideshow of photos, including the one I took of Jason at the balloon fiesta. Every time it appeared in the rotation, I remembered sitting in the damp grass, talking about marriage, about *someday*. I preferred watching the slideshow to looking at his body, laid out in the coffin. Someone had dressed him in a crisp pink button-up I knew he would have hated, and I could see how much makeup he was wearing, and the stitches holding his lips shut.

During the service, his mom invited me and Lisa to sit coffin-side with the family, like two widows. His best friend, Callista, was also with us, and she passed me Kleenex from her purse every time I needed more. She and Jason had met in a chat room when they were young teenagers, and they'd hung out when Jason visited his dad in Illinois every summer. I met Callista at the movie theater where she was a manager, before we moved to

Albuquerque. She and Jason had a very close, loving friendship, like siblings. She was his sidekick, his confidante, someone who always bailed him out of trouble. I used to wonder if she dreamed of someday being with Jason romantically, but my jealousy of his relationships with other women held me back from ever asking.

The pastor spoke about how sad it is to lose a child. I don't remember her exact words, because although she seemed like an incredibly kind person, I found it hard to concentrate on anything she was saying. *He wasn't my child*, I thought. *He was somebody's child, but he wasn't mine.* He was a man that I loved.

"Jason would have hated how much money everyone spent on these flowers," Lisa whispered. We agreed he would rather they'd have spent that money on him when he was alive. He had always been broke, constantly losing this job or that one, asking his family for money if they were speaking to him, and if they weren't, asking us, the girlfriends.

"And now a song," the pastor said, and I heard the first dreamlike notes of "Pure Imagination." While Gene Wilder sang, I sat in disbelief. *This* is the song they chose to play at his funeral? Who chose this? I felt like the entire funeral program was planned by someone who'd never met Jason. I wanted to hijack the stereo and play "Ring of Fire" by Johnny Cash.

During the song, Callista leaned over. "Jason would only listen to this song if he was *high*," she said, and I giggled into my Kleenex, relieved that I wasn't the only one who thought this was completely inappropriate.

I was dreading the moment when the pastor would conclude her speech and turn the podium over to us, the ones who had actually lost him, because I had not yet thought of anything I wanted to say. I needed more time to conjure a thoughtful sentiment, something that would do honor to his memory and still satisfy the part of me that raged at him for dying, for doing yet another horrible thing to me.

You always play the victim in your stories, I could hear him saying. *All you do is tell everyone the bad things about me.*

That's not true.

Name one thing. Name one good thing.

I decided to let the others speak first, while I waited for inspiration to strike, for a beautiful memory to plant itself in my brain and shoot its tendrils out my mouth. After his half brother said a few words without crying, I felt deeply impressed. The lap of my dress was a basket of crumpled tissues. Then Callista approached the podium and said something honest and funny and kind. I waited for a third speaker, but no one stood.

I scanned the room in a panic. His dad wasn't going to say anything? Neither was his mom? That was it? Jason was going to be buried with only two memories to take with him?

I felt my heart lodge in my throat like a plum. I stood up. I still hadn't thought of anything to say, but I had a backup plan.

"Hi," I said. "I'm one of Jason's ex-girlfriends."

At this everyone laughed, including a row of Hell's Angels up front, there to mourn the death of a rider. Their laughter made my hands shake, and it would be months before I realized that everyone was laughing at the words *one of.*

"I want to read this letter from my dad, who couldn't be here today. . . . He and Jason got along really well." I didn't know where Victor was sitting, and I didn't look for him in the crowd. I read the e-mail off the screen of my BlackBerry in an unwavering stage voice, comfortable delivering lines that I didn't write.

I became acquainted with Jason through Leigh, when they were living in Chicago. She always spoke of this young man who was very intelligent and witty and who could make her laugh. I was rather curious about "this Jason" and had the opportunity to meet him about five years ago. She was absolutely right. When he walked (bounded) into a room, the room filled with electricity. He was very animated, energetic, and had a keen sense and love for animals. If he saw one of our Cats he would speak affectionately and make up silly names for this animal. He would also cradle them in his arms. He certainly loved animals, and they loved him. He was also a very good conversationalist at the dinner table.

At the dinner table, the first night Jason met my parents, he told my dad, "I love sleeping with your daughter." I almost stabbed myself with my fork. He'd blushed and tried again: "I mean . . . sleeping . . . next to your . . ." Luckily, my dad laughed and he relaxed.

Another one of his wonderful traits was impersonating various television personalities. My daughters were locked into some of the reality shows and I always had many laughs when Jason was able to pull off a perfect impersonation of Tim Gunn or Johnny Cash. I also remember when he and Leigh moved to New Mexico and the wonderful, silly artifacts he brought back from Albuquerque, including a toy alligator and straw cowboy hats. That was true Jason. He had a very keen sense of humor and after a long day his humor and energy was a tonic for the soul.

The toy alligator lives on a bookshelf in my old bedroom at my parents' house. I don't know where he got it, or how it came to be mine, or why it's still there.

I saw a young man filled with many great traits, intelligence, wit, a great sense of humor, very adept at working with his hands, and with a love of animals. He had so much promise with so many great skills and intelligence. He is survived by friends and family who will continue to believe in him and carry his zestful spirit every day. I know I will.

Thank you, Jason, for helping me laugh and look at the World in a little different way. Godspeed, my Friend.

I made it to the end of the letter mostly without crying, then lost it at *World*. I still find the way my dad capitalizes common nouns—*Cats*, *World*, *Friend*—to be almost unbearably poignant. I'm the writer in the family, but he's the sentimentalist. "Your dad's just a simple guy," Jason used to say, in admiration. He used to call him *B-Rad* for *Brad. Be rad.*

Outside, after the funeral service, I saw Jason's grandfather. He was now a widower. His wife, the woman who'd hugged me in the parking garage, had died of cancer a couple of years after I'd met her. His body was shrunken, but his face looked enormous. His nose looked like a caricatured replica of Jason's. I noticed that his hands were shaking on top of his cane. I thought either he was in shock, or that he didn't quite know what was going on.

"Hi," I said gently, "I don't know if you remember me, but we met in Las Vegas at Victor's wedding. You and your wife took us out to lunch. I'm very sorry for your loss."

I don't know why I kept talking. He just stared at me, trembling, until I walked away. There was that vertigo again—the feeling that I might be the only one alive who remembered that afternoon in Las Vegas at all.

Callista and I piled into Lisa's car, and she drove us to the cemetery. The Hell's Angels led the cavalcade through North Little Rock, and as we followed I noticed that Lisa was blowing through one red light after another. I knew she was upset, so I didn't say anything. Eventually it dawned on me that we were part of a funeral procession; we were supposed to go through the red lights. I'd forgotten what we were doing, where we were going.

At the cemetery, Victor's girlfriend told me and Lisa that she felt Jason was with them the previous evening at dinner: across the street from the restaurant she'd seen a parked motorcycle with a white helmet on the seat, "like an angel." Then she began to cry. I could tell she was trying to connect with us and share our grief, but I didn't want to share with her. I didn't think she deserved a piece of what Lisa and Callista and I felt. For the past year, she and Victor were out of his life. Completely. Jason would have wanted me to hate her, so I did him a favor.

Toward Victor, my feelings were more complicated. I felt empathy—we both had finally reached our limits with Jason before he died—but also tremendous pain on Jason's behalf, to have had the person in his life he admired most of all cut him off. I asked Victor if he was going to be at the luncheon at Jason's grandmother's house, so we could talk more.

"No," he said, "I can't be around those people," referring to his ex-wife of almost twenty years and her family.

Like son, like father: everything had to be on their own terms. Before we left for the luncheon, I told Victor that the novel I wrote in Albuquerque would be published in a few months, and I was going to dedicate it to Jason.

He stared at me and blinked a few times. I don't think he even remembered.

Channel Georgia

(2008)

Our six-month lease in Albuquerque would be up in the middle of February, and we had no plans to renew it. Although neither of us would have ever flat-out said *this didn't work*, Jason and I each surrendered to the struggles that had sprung from our adventure. I no longer had anything in the bank, and I was spending each of my days in a heavily medicated fog; he was homesick for Chicago and Callista. We fell into the same trap that had gotten us here: *Wouldn't everything be better if we lived somewhere else?* With my savings gone, I would have to move in with my parents yet again. Jason would move in with his dad, who had agreed to pay our moving expenses. I hated accepting his money, but at the same time I reassured myself it was only fair, as I'd been supporting his son for six months.

I made all the to-do lists: *rent the truck, clean the bathtub, get the hole in the bathroom door shaped like Jason's fist fixed*. I was too depressed to write, but I was thinking of going back to school and finishing my bachelor's degree. Instead of spending my days making things up, I read admissions information, marked dead-lines in my calendar, researched CLEP exams. I told myself that this time I would follow the rules. I would make all the right choices. I e-mailed someone in the admissions department at Northwestern's night school program for working adults, forget-ting that this was where my mom finished her own bachelor's degree in the late seventies, while working full-time as a secretary at Sears. Maybe subconsciously I thought that I could be forgiven for leaving, for letting someone hurt me, for failing to prove this love was worth the pain, if I stopped trying so hard to be myself, and tried to become a little more like the woman who'd raised me.

Clearly I was a flop in the role of the carefree rebel, so I could try playing the good, obedient daughter instead: live at home, go back to school, get a job, hang out at the mall, be normal. If there was a character in between "good girl" and "bad," I didn't know who she was. I worried I would have to always vacillate between the two extremes. I was too ambitious to allow my life to become a total disaster, yet still too hungry for experience to commit to settling down in suburbia. I was also twenty-three years old. I'm sure a lot of young women feel, or have felt, as I did, but I didn't know any of them, except in books.

When she was twenty, Sylvia Plath spent a summer work-ing at *Mademoiselle* in New York City, the setting for her future novel *The Bell Jar*. On her last night at the Barbizon Hotel for Women, Sylvia got drunk and threw all her slips and sheaths and stockings off the roof. She had to borrow a peasant skirt and blouse from a friend to wear home the next day. For the rest of the summer, her plan was to sunbathe and study Joyce for her senior thesis at Smith. From a hotel roof to reading *Ulysses* in

Wellesley, from your buzzed brain saying *fuck it* to your morning brain telling you to buckle down—these extremes I knew very well.

With the deadline of our move on the horizon, Jason and I spent our January days making up for lost time, trying to fit as much of the scenery in our mental suitcases as we could, before we had to say good-bye to the Land of Enchantment. Like a child of divorce, the state itself became symbolic of our past affection and devotion to each other.

On a day trip, we drove south to Alamogordo, along what was often a two-lane highway with no other cars in sight, no cell phone reception for miles, just the occasional pay phone booth or picnic bench with a view of roadside creosote and faraway mountains. We passed Trinity Site, where the first nuclear bomb was detonated in 1945, and I took a picture of the sign that marked the spot of "the beginning of the nuclear age." We pulled over at a petrified lava plain called the Valley of Fires, and I took photos from the road of Jason standing below, his arms outstretched like wings against the black trenches, the sun casting a shadow like a scarecrow behind him. The recreation area where we'd stopped was on the east side of the Carrizozo Malpais, which translates in Spanish to "badland." In the tiny town of Carrizozo we stopped at a restaurant called Restaurant, which had green chile cheeseburgers, and bought big plastic bottles of cherry cider to take home with us. Lava fields and cherry cider: enough to make a dot on a map a destination.

I don't remember what we talked about, or how I felt on this trip. The day plays behind my eyes like someone else's silent movie: a guy in the driver's seat blowing cigarette smoke and shifting gears, a girl in the passenger seat watching out the window as the scenery goes by. If I had to guess, we probably had the same conversation we'd been having for weeks, trying to solve for the variable that made our life together unsustainable. Was it money? We never had enough, but it was hard to say where it all went. Was it the distance from our friends and family? I thought that was part of moving all the way out here, to prove we could do this without them. Was it me? Was I crazy? Impossible to live with? I stopped smoking pot, and then I tried to cut back on my alcohol consumption, too. "I remember the fun Leigh, who used to drink half a bottle of wine a night," Jason teased. The antidepressants, the sobriety—nothing I tried to heal myself with made a difference because, according to Jason, I had bipolar disorder and just wouldn't admit it. "Good luck to whoever dates you next," he told me. The variable we never found, the possibility we never debated, was that it was Jason who made our life together unsustainable.

At White Sands National Monument in Alamogordo, I took a video of him rolling down a white sand dune, the blue horizon the constant behind the velocity of his body. The largest gypsum dune field in the world, White Sands sits in a basin in the middle of the desert. After it rains, the wet gypsum crystallizes on the surface as it dries, and then erosion breaks the crystals into sand, which the wind blows into towering, shape-shifting dunes that look like they're from another planet. Spiky yucca plants grow from the sand, their long thin necks angling for more sun.

At the crest of another dune, we met a family of three in the midst of traveling around the Southwest, living out of their cargo van and homeschooling their little boy, who was sliding down the dune on a round snow sled. *Will their son someday remember this?* I wondered, watching him play with Jason and their little dog in the sand. I never forgot that day. Why do I have so many clear, detailed memories of days spent with Jason, when other memorable days of my life are so fuzzy? Maybe I never took enough care to memorize those other days. I have gone back and relived my life with Jason so many times that, in spite of all the dark and painful parts, some moments will always bloom like flowers in the fastidiously tended garden of my memory.

On another day trip, we went to the Georgia O'Keeffe Museum in Santa Fe. I didn't know much about Georgia or her work. Even though I'd seen "Sky Above Clouds" at the Art Institute of Chicago many times, I always paid more attention to the Impressionists. I hadn't yet become a lover of the sky.

At the little museum in Santa Fe, we watched a short documentary on Georgia that told me everything I needed to know to become her devotee: Midwestern-born, lover of the Southwest, part-time New Yorker, Georgia was ferociously independent, even when sharing a life with the powerful man who helped to launch her career. As hyperbolic as it sounds, I thought of Jason as my Stieglitz, because he was one of the first people to believe me when I said I was a writer, and of course I projected myself on screen as Georgia. It seemed we had so much in common, and yet she was so tough, so true to herself, that the more I learned about her, the more I wanted to resurrect her from the dead so she could teach me how to live.

In the gift shop, I bought Roxana Robinson's 656-page biography of O'Keeffe, which immediately became my combination of a devotional and a self-help book. The first hundred pages I hesitantly marked with only small translucent sticky arrows, but after that I was underlining full paragraphs in black ink. Today, when I look back at what I underlined, I can see I was trying to collect all the things I had in common with the artist, while at the same time I was searching for advice, trying to teach myself a lesson: more of this, less of that; above all, *channel Georgia.*

Page twenty-nine: "Privacy and solitude would continue to be of immense importance to Georgia throughout her life. 'I don't take easily to being with people,' she said."

Page thirty-one: "Georgia was not by nature a rebel; she did not define herself through opposition."

Page forty-six: "'I am going to live a different life from the rest of you girls,' Georgia told her high school classmates at graduation. 'I am going to give up everything for my art.'"

In an essay that celebrates the artist for her hardness, Joan Didion writes, "Like so many successful guerrillas in the war between the sexes, Georgia O'Keeffe seems to have been equipped early with an immutable sense of who she was and a fairly clear understanding that she would be required to prove it." I felt like I had a tiny spark of this inside me, the notion that I would put my art first and that made me who I was—after all, we'd moved to New Mexico so I could write a novel—but I relied too much on Jason for the oxygen that would make that spark a flame; if he doubted my work, or said negative things about my lack of productivity, the spark cooled and died.

In the spring of 1917, when Georgia was twenty-nine, she fell for the handsome, younger photographer Paul Strand (Stieglitz was his mentor). At the time, Paul was merely one of a few men taken by Georgia's charms, and she unapologetically avoided committing to any of them. In a letter to Paul, she wrote:

> *I some way seem to feel what [men] feel—never wanting to give it all. . . . As I see it—to a woman [commitment] means willingness to give life—not only her life but other life—to give up life—or give other life—Nobody I know means that to me—for more than a moment at a time. . . .*
>
> *It's always aloneness—*
> *I wonder if I mind.*

I minded. And I hated that I did. I was scared of living without Jason, but I was also scared of sacrificing my whole self to our doomed endeavor. I felt submerged in our relationship, like I was underwater and unable to delineate the outlines of my limbs. It was all blurry, without boundaries. The story I told myself of our adventure in the Land of Enchantment—that it was the result of my independent spirit, my own choices—seemed delusional when I honestly examined how controlled I was by Jason, how I'd made my life dependent on his conditional love. And yet, as much as I looked to Georgia's letters to teach me how to be independent, I was also comforted by glimpses of her vulnerability. In the summer of 1917, she wrote to Paul from Colorado, describing Stapps Lake:

> *One lake . . . surrounded by bare mountains—bare banks—rocks—a cold bare lake sparkling in the moonlight—*
> *Gosh it was bare—*
> *And I wanted to like some one tremendously—some one that liked what I saw—like I liked it.*

I wanted a witness, too. Maybe I was scared that it wouldn't matter what I did with my life if I had no one at my side to watch me do it.

A night or two before we moved back to Illinois, our neighbor Diane, who had taught me to drive, and her husband, Ted, came over. Diane helped me clean the apartment until it looked like we had never lived there at all (aside from the bathroom door, which had to be replaced). Then we all went to Del Taco. Diane had good news to share: she was pregnant and had just come from the doctor, who gave her a tiny plastic replica of a fetus, to show what she was carrying inside her. It was the size of the tip of Diane's thumb. She kept taking the tiny fetus out of the pocket of her jeans to hold in her palm and marvel at it.

As we said our good-byes, I wished I had something to give these nice people, to thank them for their help and friendship, but truthfully I hadn't anticipated feeling so close to them as I did that last night. Maybe because he'd grown up bouncing from one city—one set of parents—to another, Jason quickly made friends (or enemies) and could drop them just as easily. In Albuquerque I followed his lead. We met so many people, but Rick and Vicky were the closest thing we had to friends, and they hadn't spoken to us in months. In hindsight, I recognize how isolated I was.

Diane, now a mother of three, is one of the few people I've kept in touch with from that time. Years after I left Albuquerque, she sent me a message on Facebook that revealed her one regret: "I just wish that I had been able to give you better advice/

talk to you more about the abuse." *The abuse.* I didn't know that was what it was. Or maybe I did know, some of the time, but it was knowledge that was easy to cast doubt upon and discredit. After all, I wasn't coming into work covered in bruises like Stephanie. The cops weren't showing up at our door. I didn't think the domestic violence posters at the medical clinic applied to me. I never would have called a hotline. The closest I came to identifying what was happening was in the e-mail I sent Julia from Albuquerque: *Sometimes I feel like we are in a romantic relationship, but it is a bad, abusive kind that I should get out of.* That *sometimes* flickered on and off like electricity in a storm.

My favorite Georgia O'Keeffe painting is *From the Faraway, Nearby.* I can never decide what I love more: the image itself, or the poetry in the title. It's an oil painting of an animal skull, framed by pearly gray antlers that reach like live tendrils toward the blue southwestern sky. Below, the sherbet-colored mountain ridges are diminutive in comparison to this surreal animal that seems at once dead and alive. The title plays with this distortion of perspective, setting the skull dramatically in the foreground, afloat like a spectre that demands our gaze.

Death always seems so faraway, something that only happens to other people, until it comes so near to us it obliterates our sky.

And violence, too, seemed so faraway to me that I never recognized it in the foreground of my life with Jason.

⚡

It was warm enough for short sleeves the day we loaded the truck. We drove through Amarillo again, this time without stopping, and through the long, lackluster length of Oklahoma and into

Missouri. It got colder and colder and colder. In my overnight bag, I had packed white pillowcases we could substitute for the scratchy ones at a Microtel outside Joplin. Our last night together fell on Valentine's Day. We did not have sex, and I cried myself to sleep on the familiar pillowcase, waiting in vain for him to figure out that was what I wanted.

The next morning, we stopped at an enormous roadside souvenir depot with a glittering marquee called Ozark Village, and Jason bought me the ninety-nine-cent fake turquoise ring that I would one day wear to his funeral. The only finger it fits is my ring finger.

The previous August, our drive to Albuquerque had been so colored by hope and ambition and audaciousness. The return trip was just the opposite, darkened by trepidation and hopelessness.

When we got back to the western suburbs of Chicago, we parked the truck overnight on a side street around the corner from my parents' house, and I remember sitting in the cab, not wanting to get out, not wanting to go inside, not wanting to go backward or forward, not wanting to get on with anything.

Around midnight, I finally climbed down from the truck, and my leg went through a foot of dirty snow piled at the curb. The night sky was steel gray with light pollution and there were no stars to see. Jason and I hadn't officially broken up, but we weren't officially together either. As much as he'd hurt me, I could still point to the kind, softer parts of Jason—the sweet way he was around children or the elderly, or funny love notes he'd written me addressed to "Kit," short for *kitten*—as evidence that it was only a matter of time before he grew up and became a kind, responsible, hardworking person.

My mom could see no future. "Let him find his next victim," she said, and that was the first time I understood that that was how she saw me.

This was the fourth time I'd returned home to live with my parents since I'd originally left for New York City in 2003. In rational moments, I agreed with my mom; I knew I had to move on from Jason if I wanted any kind of future, but life felt devastatingly boring without him, and I was always only a phone call away, available for smoking pot or having sex or picking him up in the middle of the night when he was wandering snowy suburbia without socks on. Every few days, I saw him, then quit him. Then saw him again. It was a dark and dull winter.

February 29, 2008—It felt so good to see Jason again, to touch him, and have him kiss my hair. But now here I am, twenty-four hours later, desperate to hang out with him and keeping the phone nearby. Callista doesn't have to worry about being replaced. I do. I will be. Yesterday I asked him where those lips had been and he said, "Nowhere." He said, "Do you know how many opportunities I've had to have sex with girls this week and I haven't?" I said, "Wrong thing to say." He said, "No, no, no, forget it," and undid my jeans.

March 2, 2008—We'll count today as my first day of sobriety. Drug/alcohol sobriety at least. I'm also addicted to Jason and my cell phone, which I keep turned on at all times, even during the night, anxiously awaiting some desperate phone call from him that's an apology or a plea or a confession.

I cringe now when I read my diary entries from that time: how badly I wanted to find the perfect combination of responsibility and recklessness that would make a relationship with Jason tenable, and at the same time how badly I wanted to cut him out of my life completely, be strong enough to avoid texting or calling him, how much I hated myself for still wanting him. Without him, I had nothing. No money, no job, no college degree, no apartment, no car. I had my family, but we were tied together in a three-legged race; now I couldn't get anywhere without them, and at the same time I resented being hobbled by the tie.

I could borrow my parents' Saturn for the day if I drove my mom to the train station in the morning, and as soon as I could, I went to a temp agency. They gave me a proficiency exam, which required me to find misspelled words on a worksheet and take a typing speed test. When my scores came out of the printer, the manager told me I had scored higher than anyone they'd ever tested and that he had the "perfect" opportunity for me. This was the best news I'd gotten in a while.

It was a job working in a windowless call center, answering phone calls from people whose basements had flooded, and dispatching crews to install sump pumps. Not only was this winter dark and dull, but it was rainy. The phones rang off the hook. There was no lunch break. When it was busy, I had to try to flag down the woman in charge of booking the crews. Usually she ignored me because I was a temp, and so the customers on my line grew increasingly frustrated with me. This was my perfect opportunity? When the phones stopped ringing, at least I could read a book. That winter, I only wanted to read true stories about terrible lives. I read about the trials of one of the Lost Boys of Sudan, and about a girl tortured at a religious reform school in the Dominican Republic. I read about fundamentalist Mormons, child brides, and murder. At my mom's suggestion, I started reading *Eat, Pray, Love*, and literally threw it on the floor during the first chapter because although I could relate to the suffering of many, I could not sympathize with someone who found herself unhappy in spite of having the house, the career, and the husband of other people's dreams.

One day, a coworker saw me reading and looked over her shoulder nervously. "I don't think you're allowed to do that," she said.

"Do what?"

"Right, Cheryl?" She brought in reinforcements.

"But no calls are coming in," I said.

"If you really need to read something, I think you could read the product manual."

The other woman agreed. "Yeah, she could read the product manual."

I ignored them. When my boss came over and asked if I could help with some filing, I said sure. I wasn't being deliberately disobedient by reading a book. I just didn't have anything to do. When I was finished filing, I went back to my cubicle and picked up my paperback. From across the room my manager caught my eye, pantomimed holding a book, and then shut it, shaking his head.

I quit.

I was expecting a few hundred dollars from our security deposit on our Albuquerque apartment, so I thought I'd be okay for another couple of weeks, until I found a new job. Then I learned that our landlord not only charged us for replacing the bathroom door but also took excessive cleaning and repair fees from our security deposit, leaving hardly anything to return. On the Internet, I found out this was illegal and spent days making phone calls, writing what I thought were strongly worded e-mails, and talking to people on the Duke City Fix message boards, trying to get more of my money back. The apartment complex's "independent" legal team reviewed my claims and found that I was due nothing more. The next time I saw Jason, he told me he was proud of me for fighting my case, but for the first time, I wasn't doing this to impress him—I was fighting for money that belonged to me because, in a bigger sense, I wanted my life to belong to me again.

Then my parents announced that we would be taking a family vacation to Albuquerque.

"Is this a joke?" I said.

It was not a joke.

"I just lived there for six months and you never came to visit me," I reminded them.

"It would have been too hard to come when you were living with Jason," my mom said.

If I felt a pinch of self-pity that she and my dad hadn't done more to save me from Jason, this vacation made the pinch a punch. They'd waited for my relationship to end so that we could all have a "nice time." The plan was to fly into Albuquerque, visit Santa Fe and my aunt in northern New Mexico, and then drive on to Colorado, to see my dad's college buddies. I could show them around Albuquerque, but show them what? *On your left is Old Town, where Jason and I fought about who screwed up the directions on how to get to Old Town and he threatened to leave me in the supermarket parking lot. To your right, the hot air balloon fiesta field, where he promised he'd marry me someday.*

In the middle of all of this—quitting my stupid temp job, losing my battle with the apartment complex, preparing to play tour guide for my parents to a sad and strange chapter of my life—my friend Julia, to whom I'd sent all those sad dispatches from the Southwest, e-mailed me. Her boss, the cover editor of the *New Yorker*, was looking for a new assistant and asking Julia if she knew anybody. She wrote, *I kept saying no because I don't know anyone around here but LEIGH MOVE TO NEW YORK AND WORK THAT JOB.* The e-mail ended with, *Do it.*

But I did not see this as an exciting opportunity; I saw it as a prospect too terrifying to even seriously consider. I replied to Julia with a list of all the reasons why I could not *do it*: there were some days where I literally could not leave my bed, I didn't know Photoshop, I didn't have a bachelor's degree, and anyway I was planning to go back to school, so this was a bad time.

Julia called and tried to persuade me to try. "I found out the salary and it isn't a lot, but there's tuition reimbursement! You could still go back to school!"

I burst into tears. "But I'm too depressed to move to New York right now."

"Okay, okay," she said, backing off. "You don't have to move to New York, but can you at least send her your résumé?"

"And anyway, even if I did get the job, where would I live?"

"You'd live on my futon."

I said I would think about it. Then I called Jason.

"Are you crazy? This is your dream. You have to do it," he said. I told him I would think about it, hung up, and watched myself cry in the bathroom mirror. No one else was going to feel sorry for me, just because I was scared of this, so I had to feel sorry for myself. How could I reconcile Jason's support for this leap with the fact that taking the leap would mean moving farther away from him?

Over dinner, my parents expressed skepticism over the whole thing, as if this—like the savings I'd spent moving to the desert to write the novel I hadn't even finished—were another one of my far-fetched schemes that would end in disaster. "*The New Yorker?* The magazine?" My dad had gotten me a subscription for Christmas, and getting my new issue each week from the mailbox was one of the things I'd looked forward to in Albuquerque.

What was I so afraid of? I was afraid it was too good to be true. I was afraid that it *was* true, my dream, and that I would fail at it, spectacularly. I was afraid of leaving Jason, even as I wrote diary entry after diary entry about how I had to quit him. I was afraid that I didn't deserve to be saved like this.

In her essay on O'Keeffe, Joan Didion tells an anecdote about taking her seven-year-old daughter to the Art Institute. When the girl sees the cloud painting, she wants to know who created it. "I need to talk to her," she says.

So did I. *What would Georgia do?*

My parents' skepticism, combined with my own self-doubts and fear, had helped me to set my expectations so exceedingly low that it was almost like playing dress-up in someone else's clothes, dashing off my résumé and cover letter to Françoise Mouly about what a great opportunity it would be to work for her. I wrote that I wanted to relocate to New York, and by writing it down I almost believed it myself.

As soon as she read my e-mail, she called me and asked if I'd fly out to meet her. I said sure because I was still playing make-believe. My parents bought me a plane ticket and a new pair of shoes. Julia was out of town, but I crashed with an old friend who lived in the West Village. On the morning of my interview, I tried to put together a costume for an art editor's assistant, and dressed in hot pink tights, high-waisted striped shorts, and a periwinkle trench coat with cropped sleeves. Then I walked to Françoise's SoHo apartment building, where she ran an independent comic book publisher on the first floor. When she greeted me by kissing my cheeks, I fumbled the order (right first, then left) and she said, "I'm French. You'll get used to it." She was Parisian thin, with curly dark hair and thick kohl liner on her bottom lids only. Her long fingers were covered in rings, and she wore a watch that her husband, Art Spiegelman, had made, with an image from *MAUS* on the face.

I'd brought a three-ring binder with my "portfolio," which consisted of poetry chapbooks and photos of plays I'd directed, but Françoise didn't look at any of it. She just talked to me for two hours, asked if I could start by stuffing envelopes and, when I said yes, put me to work. My new shoes were too tight and my feet bled through my pink tights, but I didn't care; the bloody feet were part of the fairy tale. I was in a SoHo loft, surrounded by artwork and floor-to-ceiling bookshelves, mailing comic books to librarians. Françoise paid me for my time, and then we made a deal that I would go on vacation with my parents and then fly back to New York and start working for her full-time.

And that's what I did. I flew from New York back to Chicago, saw Jason, and, like the addict that I was, swore to myself that this would be the last time. We smoked pot outside on his dad's patio and had sex upstairs. I had glimpsed a vision of what my future in New York could look like—the cobblestone street setting of SoHo, the sweet smell from the honey-roasted nut pushcarts along Broadway, the customary cadence of *stand clear of the closing doors, please*—but more important, Françoise saw me in that future.

As Jason fucked me he whispered, *God, Leigh, I love you so much*, and I dared myself to see what would happen if I said nothing in return. Over the past year he had tried to convince me that I was too depressed, too dependent on my parents to ever do what I wanted to do, but now I had proof that he was wrong. *I don't care that you love me*, I thought. *I'm getting out of here.*

With my family I flew from Chicago to Albuquerque, and hiked up the Petroglyph Monument, covered in symbols I didn't understand. We drove to my aunt's double-wide in Questa and listened to the wind howl in the flat land at the base of the Taos Mountains, and then north to Estes Park, Colorado, where I got sick from the altitude. From Denver I flew solo back to New York. The family vacation was like the purgatory I had to pass through, to be forgiven for putting my obsession with Jason ahead of their concern and my own well-being, before I could ascend to the heaven of Manhattan.

For the first month, I slept on Julia's futon in Harlem and took the A train to Canal Street every morning to work out of Françoise's loft. When her assistant at the *New Yorker* moved on that summer, I had an awkward interview with a beautiful woman in a pristine silk blouse in HR at Condé Nast, during which I had to admit I didn't have a bachelor's degree, and she had to admit that Condé didn't actually require one.

I would work for Françoise for five years, stuffing envelopes, packing artwork, taking meeting notes, answering phone calls from famous cartoonists, carrying home free books from the piles of review copies the magazine had no use for. Eventually I wrote press releases, handled foreign rights contracts, edited comic books, and pitched them at sales conferences in Boston. I saw the Georgia in Françoise, a woman who put work above all else, and Françoise saw the Georgia in me. I was eager to be helpful, adept at learning whatever skill I lacked, and willing to work harder than anyone else to prove that I deserved to be there. On my own time, I started writing my novel again. When it was published in 2012, Françoise gave me a month off from work to go on tour.

Georgia's biographer writes, "O'Keeffe believed that work was the antidote for unhappiness, that in fact it was the only way to real happiness and fulfillment."

When I thanked Julia years later for giving me the opportunity that changed my life, she said that 60 percent of it was because she knew I was the perfect person for the job, and 40 percent of it was to get me away from Jason.

A Cinderella story in reverse: saved from worrying about the prince, the girl gets put to work.

New Territory

(2009)

I was at home in Brooklyn one January night when I heard that my acting conservatory classmate Julian had been killed in a roadside bomb blast in Afghanistan. He was twenty-five years old, and one of the first combat soldiers to die during the Obama presidency. His death was also the first I learned of from a Facebook wall.

> *Jan 23, 2009*
> *Julian commented on his own photo. 12:15 p.m.*
> *Miss you too brother. I'll be home before you know it.*

> *Jan 23, 2009*
> *X wrote at 11:42 p.m.*
> *JB baby any word on your care package?*
> *I'm glad you are safe. Just bought a book about the Tankers in the USMC during WW2. It appears the Japanese feared Marine tanks more than anything else.*
> *Home soon bro. :-)*

Jan 24, 2009
Y wrote at 6:36 a.m.
Hello old friend, I miss you buddy and am so glad I
stumbled upon your profile and have added you. I hope to
catch up and talk soon. I also really hope you are well . . .
cheers

January 24, 2009
Z wrote at 8:34 p.m.
It is with great sadness that I share that Julian was
killed in Afghanistan yesterday. Our hearts are broken . . .
I will post again when we know funeral details. Please
contact my husband if needed.

Following that, there were hundreds of comments from friends and family, an outpouring of grief and gratitude. To Julian, many wrote things they'd probably never had the chance to say in person. *Thanks for saving my life in middle school*, someone wrote. *I'll never forget that dance we choreographed*, wrote another. Who were these messages for? Were they really for Julian, or were they the kind of anecdotes told at funerals, to offer brief comfort to the bereaved? I wasn't sure. I watched new posts flood in with a morbid fascination, but I never posted anything. I had a memory of Julian, too, but if I wrote it down I thought I would have to admit I believed that Julian could still hear us.

The memory I didn't know how to turn into a Facebook post was this:

The last time I saw Julian was at school, years before, when he acted in *Bury the Dead* by Irwin Shaw. The play is set "two years into the war that is to begin tomorrow night." It is about six dead soldiers who refuse to let themselves be buried, who rise from their graves to declare the futility of war.

Even though we were never very close, I still found Julian's death shocking and shattering—he was the first person I knew who was around my age when he died. At the same time, I felt more like an observer of grief than a participant. I never posted a message to Julian on Facebook, but I did copy the words of others from his wall and paste them into an entry on my own blog, for strangers to read. Was this just a way to have a one-woman show, instead of joining the chorus of voices on Facebook? Or did I think that posting to my own blog was like talking on the phone with the door closed—that he wouldn't be able to hear what I said on the other side? (*Not that he can hear us*, I had to keep reminding myself.) In the short amount of time between learning of his death, trying to think of what to say, and finally copying the words of others to paste into my own frame, I had moved from being shaken by the loss to being shaped by how I had *encountered* the loss.

This was new territory. The message boards and listservs and blogging communities where I'd spent my adolescence had always been a world apart from whatever was happening in my life away from the keyboard. My online life gave me more choices, more control, more freedom. During my first year at college, in 2003, I still felt more intimate with the girls I knew only on LiveJournal than with my classmates, or even my roommate. Before I went out to my first bar ever in New York, I wrote an LJ post to ask what kind of drink I should order when I got there (Sex on the Beach). Online it was so much easier to talk, without judgment or shame, about all the dark things I wanted to talk about: anxiety and depression, loneliness and longing. Learning of Julian's death on Facebook was a collision between my digital and offline lives. Here was someone I knew, whose face and body I had watched onstage, whose death was unfolding before me in a digital territory where the borders were no longer under my control.

The summer after Julian died, I went to New Mexico on vacation again. It had been over a year since I'd gone there on vacation with my family, and the first time I would be going by myself. I found a woman on Craigslist who rented her guesthouse by the week. The ad mentioned goats, but I ignored that part. The rental was cheap and fifteen minutes outside Santa Fe. I booked my flight and rented a car.

"You're going there to write?" friends in New York asked, as if that were the only acceptable reason for going anywhere by yourself. One girlfriend even confessed she'd never eaten alone in a restaurant before.

"Yes," I said, to reassure them. I was going there to eat fish tacos and sopapillas and stare at the sky. I was going to make a pilgrimage to Georgia O'Keeffe's house in Abiquiu and soak in the hot springs at Ojo Caliente. I was going to eat in restaurants with just a book and a Corona for company. In New York I was under so much pressure to be ambitious and successful, and physically crushed by crowds during my daily commute to Times Square, it was hard not to be nostalgic for the spaciousness and possibility of the Southwest. I could go back to the place where I was nobody. That was my idea of a vacation: be nobody in the middle of nowhere.

I flew into Albuquerque, picked up my rental car, and drove north. The sun felt like a gift from someone who'd been waiting years for me to come back and pick it up. I stopped at the Trader Joe's in Santa Fe, to pick up some food for my week at the guesthouse, and as I was loading my groceries into the trunk, my phone rang. It was Jason. I hadn't spoken to him in months.

"You'll never guess where I am," I said.

"Where?"

"Santa Fe!" It felt good to say this—it felt safe. He was hundreds of miles away; what could he do?

"Did you move back there?"

"No," I said, "I'm just on vacation for a week."

In reply, he told me his girlfriend had just kicked him out of their apartment. "Now I don't have anywhere to live." The girlfriend was Lisa. Jason said he had been doing construction work under the table for a guy opening a Chinese restaurant, who'd promised to pay him at the end of the job, but then the guy had disappeared, never paid. Now he didn't have money for rent, so he and Lisa got into a fight, and she scratched and kicked him until he threatened to call the police.

I thought I remembered him telling me that Lisa went to Northwestern, but her behavior in this story didn't align with the image I had of a Northwestern student. Either my stereotype was totally off, he was lying, or she was crazy. Or, more likely, Jason had turned her crazy.

"Wait, she's a Northwestern student?"

"Yeah," he said, and continued his story. The characters were new, but the central conflict was one I'd already heard a thousand times: everyone was against him, and no one would give him a chance.

"Why don't you call your dad," I suggested, "and go stay with him?"

"Why don't I meet you in Santa Fe? Let's move back." This came up every time we spoke—the idea of a do-over. The last time I'd seen him was just a few months earlier, when I'd been in Illinois for a wedding; I went to his place after the reception, he scooped me up like a bride and carried me to bed, and we had sex. (At the time, I thought he and Lisa were broken up. At his funeral, she and I would unintentionally put the chronology together and realize they were not.) In bed, he'd said the same thing. "Let's go back." I said I was a shell of a person when we were there the first time, didn't he remember that? "Well, I guess you did cry in the bathroom a lot."

"Jason, I have a job in New York. I'm just here on vacation."

"Quit your job," he said. "You can get another job." *Yeah right,* I thought, *quit my job at the* New Yorker. Still, I was tempted. I knew that I should appreciate all that I now had: a prestigious job, a charming apartment with lovely roommates in Brooklyn, good friends, party invitations every weekend, and yet. And yet? I was single. I worked two part-time jobs to supplement my salary at the magazine, and I had started going to night school. My life didn't feel any less stressful than it had in New Mexico. It was just a more impressive kind of stress. I was the young, ambitious career woman in the big city, instead of the depressed waitress in the desert.

"I have to go," I told him. "I was just getting some groceries and now I have to drive." The lonely, nostalgic part of me wanted to stay on the phone with him, but another part of me felt fortified by sun, ready to hang up and get on with it.

"Can I at least call you later?"

I told him he could. Then I threw my cell phone in the backseat and drove to the house with the goats. It was set back at the end of a single-lane road, off a winding street where the locals let me know I was driving too slowly by speeding by in their 4x4s. In the daylight I could at least see where I was going, but at night I couldn't see each new curve ahead until the curve was already upon me, and I wasn't used to driving in a rural place in the dark. In Albuquerque, there were streetlights everywhere, but outside Santa Fe there were none. And I was alone. There was a freedom in this: no one knew where I was, and I wasn't accountable to anyone. There was danger: If something happened, who would find me? And there was the threat of my own dark thoughts: a sharp turn of the wheel and I'd be off-road, off the edge, in the middle of nowhere, gone.

Jason called back the next day to say he'd spent the night on Michigan Drive, panhandling, and it wasn't so bad—he'd try it again. Today he was going to go enlist in the air force.

"Jason, don't," I said.

"What other choice do I have?"

I thought of Julian. He was the only person I knew who'd been in the military, and now he was dead. "We're at war," I said.

"I wouldn't be deployed; that's not what the air force is. They would train me to be an engineer and work on planes and stuff."

"I have to go," I said. I was on vacation, and I had all the time in the world, but I didn't want to give any more of it to him, even if I was in a place I likely never would have discovered without him. No matter what you gave him, Jason made you feel like you still owed more.

The next morning, I left for Abiquiu, a tiny town of 230 people in northern New Mexico. Georgia O'Keeffe lived there for almost forty years, alternating between a Spanish Colonial compound that she converted with the help of a friend, and her home at Ghost Ranch, farther north. During their marriage, Alfred Stieglitz kept her tethered to him and New York for at least part of each year, and she didn't move to New Mexico full-time until after his death in 1946. Before then, she made shorter, annual trips out west, but in 1939 she had a nervous breakdown and couldn't go. To a friend she wrote, *I wish so much to go that I almost wish I had never been there.*

In my copy of her biography, this sentence is underlined in black ink.

To tour her house in Abiquiu, I had bought a ticket months in advance, by calling a phone hotline, and I was told I was lucky—I had gotten the last ticket available. On the drive, the fresh desert morning bloomed into a day that was just as bright and hot as the one that came before it. I pulled to the side of the road occasionally to take snapshots of the landscape. My cell phone received no signal. I passed almost no other cars. When I arrived at the designated spot for the tour, I saw that I had picked a tourist attraction far beyond my age demographic. Aside from the septuagenarians and me, there was a mother in her thirties, with a small, blonde daughter. The girl was wearing a red dress.

"Look, we match," I said, gesturing to my own red outfit.

"My name's Ali, what's yours?"

"Leigh."

"That's a pretty name," she said.

Ali stuck to my side throughout the tour, occasionally holding my hand. When we came to a majestic sage tree in the courtyard, I rubbed my palms over the leaves, and put them under her nose so she could smell the fresh scent.

There's a photo I love of Georgia, taken by her friend Ansel Adams. She's lying on the ground at Ghost Ranch in a painter's apron, one pale arm draped over her face to cover her eyes. It was taken in 1937. If this were a Dorothea Lange or Walker Evans portrait, we would assume this woman is lying on the ground, covering her face, out of some desperation. But I've felt that New Mexico sun. I know Georgia is lying there in bliss.

I wrote one poem in Santa Fe. It ends like this:

> *The only thing we ever had in common*
> *was making the choices that would net the best stories and*
>
> *when you called, I was back where we started, watching*
> *the sun crown the hills. I was going to ask if for the past*
>
> *two years you've been living in your memory, too, but you*
> *interrupted to say you'd enlisted, and here it was, the*
> *unimaginable*
>
> *I'd never imagined, a premonition of violence, a reason*
> *to drive until I was out of range, off the map.*

❧

In Santa Fe, I bought a book called *Women of the West*, a collection of diaries, letters, and autobiographies by nineteenth-century pioneer women, whose recollections make my life with Jason in the Southwest look like a honeymoon in St. Lucia. Take the diary of Miriam Davis Colt, the twelfth of seventeen children from a poor New York City family. In 1856, she heads west to a promising "experimental vegetarian settlement colony" in Kansas with her husband. When they arrive, they find the colony to be nothing like they expected. Everyone is living in tents "without floors or fires." Miriam fashions an Indian blanket into a door, but still "the prairie winds come whizzing in." Her husband takes two wooden boards from their covered wagon and tells her, "Miriam, you may make your bed on the smooth surface of these two boards." But she insists he take the bed because he works the hardest, and she and the children take the floor. Within months, almost her entire family is felled by disease.

A few years later, to raise money to support herself and her surviving daughter, she publishes her diaries, along with letters and poetry, in a volume called *Went to Kansas: Being a Thrilling Account of an Ill-Fated Expedition to That Fairy Land, and its Sad Results: Together with a Sketch of the Author and How the World Goes with Her.*

Illness, weather, death, and debt—Miriam wrote it all down. One entry describes how she sold her nicest clothes so that she could afford a gravestone for her son who died in the night, after calling out for bread and apples. It's totally Dickensian, yet true, and authored by a woman. *Where does that instinct come from?* I wonder, the thought process that goes, *Life is hard and terrible. I know what I'll do: I'll tell a story about it.* I think I know the answer. I think fitting an experience inside the frame of a story is how some of us survive.

I never really kept a private diary as a young adult (in a box somewhere are piles of journals with just one or two entries), not because I didn't have anything to write about, but because I couldn't envision an audience—maybe it was my acting classes that made me think I shouldn't write without one in mind. Or maybe as a teenager, it was impossible to imagine that the audience for the entries might just be *me*, years later as an adult.

But in the late nineties and early aughts, I began keeping a diary online, which was new territory. On LiveJournal, you could curate the exhibit of your life, leaving out all the boring bits, and showing, through images and words, your most original, creative self. The self you most wanted others to see, even if broken or damaged. No need to use real names or profile pictures; we knew one another as faceless personas, as diarists, and the anonymity allowed for great intimacy. We spilled secrets. We exposed our vulnerabilities. A few of these women are still my friends today, including Julia, whom I first met online when she was fifteen, taking artsy selfies in her suburban New Jersey bedroom, a Frank O'Hara poem taped to the ceiling. When I moved to New York for the first time, in 2003, we arranged to meet in person, and she lied to her parents about whom she was meeting. In my dorm room, I put on the *Funny Girl* DVD and we watched Barbra Streisand sing "My Man," with her big, elegant hands rippling against the darkened stage.

Years before I was sending confessional e-mails, or scrolling through Facebook grief, I was keeping a public diary about what it was like to be a teenage girl, on a social network where girls were queens of our own sad little kingdom, whose walls we defended by staying anonymous, changing personas if anyone threatened to encroach upon our coterie.

Women on the frontier lived in fear of being alone at night, and anything that would intrude upon the boundaries of their homesteads: animals, Indians, vagrant men displaced by the Civil War or turned out of work in the mines. Cathy Luchetti and Carol Olwell, the editors of the collected letters, write that "much of their fear . . . came from their inability to read their environment with any accuracy." They were afraid of all that they didn't yet know to be afraid of.

For some women, these fears became a chronic condition of melancholia, "an extreme depression so common that scholars today have tried to determine if it was due to a fatty diet high in salt pork, fried beef, eggs, milk, and butter, or if trace mercury found in wells dug in the mining areas might have triggered the erratic behavior of many." Mrs. Arthur Cowan, who lived in Montana, or, as she tells it, "forty miles from civilization, where nobody lives and dogs bark at strangers," kept a diary with entries such as these:

> Cold day. . . . Sid went to look for poisoned coyotes. Came back nearly froze.
>
> Cold windy day 24 below zero. Fed the sheep. Very lonesome.
>
> Dark, dreary day. And the snow is flying . . .
>
> Blustering this morning. Fed the sheep and then took them out on the hills. . . . This is a long lonely winter.

10 degrees below zero this morning. Have been very down hearted today and had a very bad headache . . .

My heart is very lonely and sad to have no one to sympathize with me. I must bear all my troubles alone.

Men are working at lambing. Oh I feel so lonely, so sad and discontented.

The same old routine over again. Running after sheep again all day. This hardly seems like living . . .

Take away the sheep and weather and these could be Live-Journal posts from 2001—not just mine, but from the other girls on my friends page, too. Girls with usernames like *thisvelocity* ("Interests: (1) trailer parks & tornadoes") and *andmilestogo* ("Name: frostbite and cigarettes"). Girls with migraines. Girls who cut. Girls who wrote poetry in gray lowercase on black backgrounds. Girls who took black-and-white self-portraits using film and tripods and timers, portraits in which their faces were always turned away. Were we mercury poisoned? Too much salt pork? I'm not saying we had it as bad as Mrs. Cowan, but empathy can come from recognition, and in her diary, the repetitive tedium of melancholy is so plainly spoken, so familiar.

On LJ, our currency was pain and we were rich. Our greatest accomplishment was turning our suffering into art. My art was poetry, and I was good at taking a scar and turning it into a story, a slight into a rallying cry.

But while LiveJournal supported my growth as a young woman and poet—by introducing me to girls like me, who were on antidepressants, girls who would also rather be at home writing poems than suffering through another day of high school—it also taught me that sadness was what made me unique and beautiful. My boyfriend in high school got on board with my identity as a tragic figure; we dated for more than two years, and he didn't mind if I cried on a daily basis. In fact, he wanted to marry me, and my mom tried convincing me this was a good idea because he was always so nice and loyal to me. A lot of people marry their childhood sweethearts, she argued. What was so wrong with that? But I was about to move to New York City. I imagined bigger things ahead, such as extremely interesting and handsome men who would all be in love with me. It didn't work out exactly as I planned it in my head, but three years after breaking up with my high school sweetheart, I met Jason.

And then after Jason and I broke up, I added the story of our relationship to my inventory of wounds. I still wanted someone to fall in love with me not in spite of my depression and past relationship drama, but *because* of these things. I would spend years wandering the streets of New York, drinking too much and turning first dates into confessionals, the jukebox in my head playing the same song on repeat: *Are you my boyfriend? Are you?* like the tragic heroine of a children's board book. I can see now why I rarely got asked for a second date.

A few months before my trip to Santa Fe, I'd had a procedure done to remove precancerous cells from my cervix after some bad biopsy results. Jason was to blame for this—he'd given me the virus that had caused the abnormal cells. The gynecologist explained that there was a low risk I'd be rendered infertile by the procedure, that I would miscarry indefinitely, that my cervix would become "incompetent." An *incompetent cervix*—I found this phrase darkly hilarious, since after putting my life back together in New York I prided myself on my competence, and here was something totally out of my control.

My mom flew in from Chicago to be with me when I had the procedure done at Beth Israel. They gave me local anesthesia, so there wasn't any pain beyond the initial shot, but I could smell myself burning as they used an electric wire that looked like an Easter egg dipper to scrape tissue from my cervix. For a week after, I bled. I waited for the lab results that would tell me whether it was a success, or if there were still more abnormal, potentially cancerous cells.

At the time I had just started dating this nice, tall guy named William. We met at a mutual friend's reading in Chinatown. The theme of the reading was "heartbreak." In between sets, they had a contest for the audience to come up and tell stories of heartbreak, for a chance to win a free drink ticket. My name was written all over this.

I went up to the mic and told the story of a boy named Taylor in my third-grade class. Taylor had a mushroom haircut and also a long, skinny tail of hair that went all the way down his back. He showed up at my house on his bike one afternoon to deliver a note that read *DO YOU LIKE ME CIRCLE ONE YES OR NO*. My mom accepted the note, while I hid upstairs in my bedroom, begging her to tell him I wasn't home. I didn't like any boys, but I would have felt too sorry for Taylor if I had to circle no, so I planned to just pretend like I'd never received the message.

The next day at school, I found out on the playground that this same note had been delivered to every girl in our class. I went from feeling special yet embarrassed, to allowing myself to be swept up in the mob of meanness and ridicule. We all laughed at Taylor, then went back to ignoring him. That day in class, he took his pair of kids' scissors and cut the web of skin between his forefinger and thumb, spilling blood over his desk. Our teacher, horrified, sent him to the nurse, and told the class he must not have taken his ADHD medication, but of course I knew the real reason he had cut himself, and felt the heat of my own culpability in his humiliation.

I won the drink. William asked for my number. If that sad story was what made him interested in me, I thought, then we were starting off on the right foot. On our first date, we got coffee at a pastry shop near the Columbia campus and watched the peacocks in the yard of the Cathedral of St. John the Divine. He told me stories about going to South Africa with his high school choir, and about driving his mom's Toyota Echo to Castle Valley, Utah, on a self-made vision quest.

"You're a liar," I said every time he said anything interesting, and this delighted him, made him laugh.

After a few rounds of this, he said, "Why do you keep saying that?"

I wasn't sure. I replayed the three words in my head, like running my tongue over the familiar point of a canine tooth. Then I realized that this was something I used to say to Jason, to provoke him into telling me which part of what he was saying was actually the truth.

"Oh, I used to date a liar," I finally said, and then forced myself not to say anything more, lest I fuck up this perfect afternoon.

We went out again, to an improv show in the village, and to the tiny food co-op where William used to work, so he could introduce me to the delicacy of the dehydrated banana (I thought they were disgusting). Then, on a Saturday afternoon that was also the first day of spring to feel like summer, he came over to my apartment in Brooklyn and I cooked dinner while he played Patsy Cline's "Walkin' After Midnight" on the Rhodes keyboard in my bedroom that I kept for a musician friend whose apartment was too small. I was wearing a sleeveless dress that buttoned up the front. Jason had undone those buttons. William undid those buttons. We fooled around in my bed until we reached the point where I was down to my underwear, and I had to stop him.

"We can't have sex. I'll explain later."

"Why can't you explain now?"

"Because then you'll stop calling me," I said.

"That's ridiculous."

"I just had surgery and I might have cervical cancer?"

"Holy shit," he said, and wrapped his arms around me, and we slept like that all night, nesting spoons.

The perfect ending to a story that began with heartbreak is that of course he did stop calling me after that. Over a week later, he sent me an e-mail to say he decided there was a "fundamental difference" between us that he couldn't name or define, but he hoped I was enjoying the beautiful weather.

As wrong for me as Jason was, I seemed incapable of finding—not finding, but *holding on to*—anyone who was better. Like an alcoholic who secretly wishes she'll become pregnant and that will force her to get sober for nine months, I wished for a boyfriend who would occupy so much of my headspace that Jason would be crowded out, exiled to a memory.

The Worst Movie I Ever Saw

(2011)

In late July, Brooklyn reeks of rotten garbage and dog shit. Twilight comes late, smoky blue. No crickets or June bugs, just sirens and the repetitive thunder of the R train below Fourth Avenue. One night, shortly after Jason's funeral, while waiting for the subway, I watched a woman pull her sweatpants down to urinate onto the tracks, and I saw intense relief on her face before I blocked my ears and forced myself to look the other way. When the train finally came, the air-conditioned car offered a brief reprieve from the smells and the heat of the station.

At Brian's apartment, I arrived to find him watching *COPS* on TV. A police officer was chasing a man in a wifebeater over fences, between houses sitting on cracked foundations, and across ugly yards. When he finally tackled the criminal in a driveway, I cringed.

"Can you please turn that off?" I asked him.

"Why?"

"It's making me upset."

"Why is it making you upset?"

"I don't know," I said. I thought I would sound too sensitive if I tried to explain that I couldn't watch desperate people who had run out of options pee in public or run from police.

Instead of changing the channel, Brian suggested I go in the bedroom until the episode was over. So I sat on the bed and fumed. If he sympathized so much with law enforcement, and I sympathized with criminals, we were doomed.

But I also didn't want to be—couldn't bear to be—alone. I didn't want to sleep in my own apartment, in the bed I'd shared with Jason six, seven, eight weeks earlier. I stayed at Brian's every night. He was a prolific sleeper and I was an insomniac. In the middle of the night or early in the morning, when Brian was asleep and I felt alone, my grief would find me.

It was grief that made me feel covetous enough to ask Lisa if she'd look for a purple throw blanket Jason had taken from me three years before, because I wanted it back. (Or did I just not want her to have it?) Grief that took my hand and led me online to look at pictures and memories of Jason on Facebook, clicking through anonymously, never commenting, always lurking. I was jealous of Callista, who seemed to always be receiving "signs" of Jason at her bartending job—a song played at his funeral on the radio; a dollar for a tip with *JASON* written on the bill in Sharpie ink.

The only thing I could count as a sign was a dream: I am standing at the bottom of a stairwell in a dark, musty basement. Someone opens the door at the top of the stairs and light pours in. It's Jason. He's standing at the top. He's come here to yell at me for letting them bury him. He was never really dead; it was all a mistake, and I'm to blame. I get the sense that he's at the top of the stairs and I'm at the bottom because he wants to trade places with me.

I woke up sweating, afraid to move.

Once I had exhausted Facebook, I would browse Craigslist for New Mexico real estate listings. Browsing was already a habit, something I'd done for years to break up the tedious afternoons at office jobs, but now, at night, my searching took on a new desperation.

I found a miner's cabin for sale on the Turquoise Trail, a 1991 Spirit Mobile Home in Pojoaque, a three-bedroom in Moriarty for less than fifty thousand dollars. I didn't have any money, but that didn't stop me from dreaming, with every listing, of abandoning my life in New York and moving back there, by myself. *I could get a dog*, I thought, before I remembered that I don't like dogs. *I could get a cat. A guard cat.* My favorite part of each listing was always the property photos because they showed the sky. When I dreamed of leaving, I never thought of my job or of Brian or what I'd tell my family. I thought of the sky alone and it made me break out in yearning like a rash.

In Albuquerque, I'd been the sleeper. Jason was always the one awake in the middle of the night. Before we'd moved, I'd done what I thought was the "mature" thing to do, and switched from using LiveJournal to Blogspot. From our new apartment in Albuquerque, I'd posted the first entry:

> *Jason woke me up at four in the morning by jumping on the bed. He was wearing his cowboy hat.*
> *Do we have any tuna left? he said.*
> *No, I said.*

If you wake up and I'm not home it's because I'm out trying to catch a stray cat.

Okay, I said.

He came home empty-handed. He said it was a little white cat, but it kept running away from him and he had to chase it through the tall prickly grass along the road near our apartment. Everyone wants to know why we would want to move to Albuquerque. Last week at a party someone laughed at us and said, "People come here going, 'Look at the pretty sagebrush,' but we call it weeds."

Those sleepless nights at Brian's were even lonelier knowing Jason wasn't out there anymore, not anywhere, not even as a friend or an enemy; there was no way to call and ask if he remembered the night he went looking for the little white cat.

I avoided posting anything to Facebook about Jason's death, but eventually I posted something on my blog, a territory whose borders I felt I could control. *Dear Jason,* I wrote, *The night before your funeral, I told your mom the story of the night you proposed to me. I'm wearing the ring you bought me in the Ozarks. It's cheap plastic, but it has veins in it like turquoise.* I signed it *Love.*

After the post went up, a few friends e-mailed their condolences. They'd had no idea. They'd had no idea because I was daunted by the task of telling them. They asked if there was anything they could do, and I replied, asking a few girlfriends in New York if they'd go to a yoga class with me. They were all too busy. *But it seems like you're handling everything really well!*

I didn't feel like I was handling anything well.

My friend Sarah took me to dinner, and I described the funeral to her: how they'd buried him in a pink shirt he would have hated, how they played "Pure Imagination" during the service, how hot it was in Little Rock. I tried to summon the details as if from a great distance, as if this was one of those sad stories that would become amusing, or at least interesting, after enough tellings. (*A Thrilling Account of an Ill-Fated Expedition to That Fairy Land, and its Sad Results!*) Maybe it looked like I was *handling everything really well* because after unsuccessfully hawking my wounds for so long, I had learned how to protect those around me from my private horror. I could save everyone the trouble of not knowing what to say to me and my grief by never running out of stories to tell.

After dinner, outside the restaurant, Sarah stared at me. I stared back. Finally she asked if it would be okay if she gave me a hug. At first, I thought I was agreeing to it for her sake, to give her something to do, but as she held me I felt overcome by how badly I wanted the embrace to continue. And I wished, impossibly, that her thin arms would be transformed into his. *But he's dead*, said a voice in my head. *But just last month you had his arms around you and you couldn't wait for him to leave so you could get back to your life*, said the voice's cruel twin.

A couple of nights later, Brian invited me to go with him to see a movie he had to cover for his job as an online news producer. I didn't really have the energy, but he convinced me to meet him at an Italian restaurant near the screening room.

"We'll make a date out of it," he said, and there seemed to be an unspoken agreement that this date would take my mind off of whatever I was, or wasn't, handling.

At dinner, I had wine, focaccia dipped in olive oil, an entrée, more wine, dessert. I felt like a slave to my appetite and wished I were wasting away instead. *Look at her! She's wasting away!* people said behind my back, in my fantasy life. What people? Friends. Coworkers. Anyone who knew I'd just been to a funeral. I wished my body could telegraph my grief for me, so I wouldn't have to try and explain what I felt but didn't yet understand.

Brian drank a Coke, and leaned in to ask if I thought they would charge him if he ordered a refill. I told him to just go for it. *Life is short!* I could have said but didn't. One of the weird things about grief is how utterly profound it feels, and yet the only things that come to mind are clichés: *he was so young; it's not fair; life is short!* When the bill finally came, Brian was right: they'd charged him for both. He paid the check. He always paid. I didn't even reach for my purse anymore. We held hands and walked to the movie.

In the screening room, the seats were plush and violet. Buzzed from the wine at dinner, I sank low into my chair, eager to leave my life behind for a couple of hours.

The movie was about two young people in love. One of them is a British citizen, and the other is American. The falling-in-love scenes were all shot through the filtered golden light of an Urban Outfitters catalog. The British citizen is so in love with the American citizen that she overstays her visa, and this causes some problems, so they have to be long-distance for a while. The plot was so banal that I started hoping for a car accident. I wanted one of the lovers to die. Maybe he could go surfing in the Pacific and drown and then she wouldn't be able to attend the funeral because she'd be far across another ocean and wouldn't that be so sad? There was no part of me that would relinquish itself to the fantasy of their romance. If the director wanted me to feel for his characters, I needed them to suffer. At the very least I wanted her to have to live in England forever, always wondering what might have been, filled with regret over how young and stupid she'd been.

But the girl's daddy hires a lawyer to fix the immigration problem so they can be together again, and the most devastating fight in the whole movie happens when one of them discovers a text message not meant for their eyes. At the end, tragedy: though they're back together, it's left ambiguous whether they're going to succeed as a couple.

My eyes sprang with tears of rage during the final credits.

"What'd you think?" Brian asked.

"That was the worst movie I ever saw."

He laughed. "Come on, no, it wasn't."

"YES, IT WAS. IT WAS THE WORST MOVIE I EVER SAW."

Brian looked around the theater, embarrassed. "Lower your voice," he whispered.

Brian and I met online in January 2011. His profile made me laugh—there was a picture of him smiling wryly next to Vanilla Ice, and another picture of him in fishing waders with a hawk on his arm. I said he'd be able to recognize me at the bar by my Pendleton blanket sweater, and he said he didn't know what that was, but he'd be wearing a Paddington Bear sweater.

At the end of our first date, he asked if I would spend his thirty-first birthday with him.

"Don't you have anyone better than me to spend your birthday with?"

"Not really," he said. "What would you want to do?"

"It's your birthday—what do *you* want to do?"

Together we devised a fantasy birthday scenario, in which we would drive to an arcade on Long Island that he hadn't been to since a Jewish summer day camp trip during his youth. A couple of days later, on his birthday, Brian pulled up in front of my apartment in a rental car. He was late, and I'd become so nervous while waiting for him that I almost canceled the date. But Brian was a good driver, and I relaxed in the passenger seat. Somewhere in the Bronx, we saw a hotel on the second floor of a storage facility, and he asked if we should pull over and start a family.

I laughed and told him that my dad was worried I'd end up in the trunk of the rental car by the end of the date.

"We'll see how it goes," Brian said.

In the arcade parking lot, I gave him a gold plastic birthday crown inlaid with plastic jewels and made him wear it. Inside, we played Skee-Ball all afternoon. I beat Brian badly at simulated boxing. We traded in our arcade tickets for Tootsie Rolls and then drove back to Brooklyn, picked up Taco Bell for dinner, and went back to his apartment, where I met his cat Kia, who was born without a tail. Together we watched *The NeverEnding Story*.

I had forgotten the movie was so dark, so sad. I hadn't watched it since I was much younger, but now I saw the swamp of sadness with its quicksand as a perfect metaphor for depression. I was dreading the future conversation with Brian, if this relationship progressed—and I was hoping it would—about my depression, and the medication I was taking. Some boyfriends got it, some didn't (one had burst out laughing when I'd used the phrase *mental illness*). I'd just started seeing a new psychiatrist, who called me *Lay-uh* and spoke to me in Hebrew until he realized I had no idea what he was saying. At my second appointment, after skimming my file, he said, "Ah, you're my depressed young woman," as if that made me singular. He gave me trazodone to help me sleep through the night.

When I eventually told Brian, in bed, in the dark, he said it was no big deal. He was on antidepressants, too. Relief was my blanket. I felt so comfortable being with him, it seemed almost too good to be true. We were seeing each other every couple of days when, after a few weeks, Brian got a strange pain in his leg.

"Maybe you slept on it funny," I said, but the feeling didn't go away. He started limping. If he couldn't get a seat on the subway, he stood and suffered in a way that made me wince in sympathy. Aside from going to work, he couldn't leave his apartment. No more dates or outings. I'd go over there, bring food or make it, do his dishes, sleep next to him, sexless. Doctors thought he had sciatica, then told him it was a herniated disc. He was supposed to do physical therapy, but felt too depressed to call and schedule the appointment. He took Percocet. We watched TV.

February passed in this way. And then March. I liked Brian, but I resented playing the role of caretaker for someone I'd only just met. I wanted him to get better, but I couldn't do it all on my own.

In addition to working for Françoise and teaching theater to children again, I was also going to school full-time, finally finishing my bachelor's degree at Brooklyn College. In April, I would get a week off from teaching and classes for spring break, and I needed a vacation. The siren song of New Mexico was always there in the back of my mind, selling itself as the antidote to my overscheduled life in New York.

On a Sunday morning, we had brunch at a diner a couple of blocks from his apartment. "I've been thinking of going on vacation," I said. "My spring break is coming up. Would you want to come with me?"

"A vacation where?"

"New Mexico."

Brian looked skeptical. "What's in New Mexico?" he asked.

"Sunshine?" I hadn't prepared a convincing speech. I couldn't explain my intense feelings for the place over eggs and home fries, and his reaction to the idea made me reluctant to even try.

"I'll just go by myself, then," I said.

He shrugged.

After that, he stopped calling. When I finally texted, he responded to let me know he thought I wanted more of a relationship than he did. Insulted, I insisted we meet in person to talk about it. I didn't think it was fair that I was taking care of his needs the way a girlfriend would, and he was scared that this was turning into a "relationship."

He agreed to meet me at a Mexican restaurant. It was April first. I was sick with a cold, and so I skipped my usual margarita. I tried to explain why I liked him so much: "You never yell at me or call me names; you've never hit me; you wouldn't cheat on me."

"All that's happened to you before?"

"I've *told* you—"

"Don't cry," Brian said, less as a comfort and more of a warning, so people wouldn't look at us. It occurred to me that the qualities I'd just listed were maybe not the best reasons for being in a relationship with someone. The only box Brian was ticking at that point was "not a horrible person."

"Do you want to come over?" he asked.

"No. I'm sick. I just want to go home."

"You're still the funniest girl I've ever met," Brian said, offering his idea of a consolation prize.

"Well," I said, "I'm not a comedian. Or a nurse."

We broke up.

I booked my trip. And like I'd said the magic words or cast the perfect spell, Jason started texting me again, out of the blue. Our lives seemed destined to collide, like outer space debris in a Hollywood movie. It was destabilizing and thrilling both: every time I thought Jason was finally out of the picture, he popped back up.

Right before spring break, the New York DMV screwed up my driver's license renewal and gave me a state ID instead of a license, so I had to cancel the car rental I had booked for my trip. I was literally back where I'd started: in New Mexico without wheels, in need of a ride everywhere.

From the airport in Albuquerque, I caught a shuttle bus to Santa Fe, where I'd rented a little vacation condo with one bedroom and a kiva fireplace. When I opened the front door, I saw a staircase. There were two bedrooms upstairs. Three bathrooms.

I called the front desk.

"I think you made a mistake," I said. "There's only one of me."

The woman laughed at me. "We upgraded you, that's all."

Being alone just reminded me of how alone I was. I heard

things at night, but only because the rest of the world was so silent, and left the light on in the hallway, something I hadn't done since I was a child. In the morning, out my west-facing window, I counted sandy peach-colored hills, dotted with green brush, and the indigo mountains beyond. The more images I memorized by Georgia O'Keeffe, the more the landscape looked as if it copied its brushstrokes from her, instead of vice versa.

On my second night, I went on a ghost tour of downtown Santa Fe. At the river, the guide told us the story of La Llorona, said she drowned herself there. At La Posada Hotel, we heard the story of the Staab family, who'd originally lived there in the nineteenth century. When Julia Staab lost her youngest baby, her hair went white and she lost her mind, never leaving her bedroom again. The guide claimed that she still haunted the halls, spooking guests and making glasses fly in the hotel bar. Jason was alive, but still I thought I knew what it felt like to be haunted. That's what our love was: a haunting.

He and I were texting and e-mailing during my New Mexico trip. I bought a bright green vintage feathered hat and sent him a picture of myself wearing it. On Easter, we spoke on the phone for seven hours. He was living with his grandmother in Little Rock, and I could hear her birds screaming in the background. "She wants to know who I'm talking to, since I never talk on the phone this long, and I told her you," he said. "Come visit."

"I'm not going to come to Little Rock."

"We'll go camping in the Ozarks."

"I'm not going camping."

We negotiated, until I persuaded him to visit me in Brooklyn in June. We agreed to split the airfare, and I considered this progress, proof of his evolution. I felt like I'd tried my best with Brian, to have a healthy, stable relationship, and in light of its failure I fell back on old standbys—our shared nostalgia, the promise of good sex, the allure of Jason's unpredictability.

Seven hours. I wish I could remember more of what we talked about, but I only remember the time passing, the effervescent pleasure I felt when I made him laugh, the way he pronounced *pin* for *pen* and *bin* for *been* and *did* for *dead*.

Two weeks before Jason was due to arrive in Brooklyn, Brian e-mailed and asked me to dinner. He apologized for how things had ended, told me his back was healed and he'd just started a new job. While he was on vacation in Italy, I had visited him in his dreams.

Last Days
(2011)

Jason arrived in New York on a Tuesday. I was at my office in SoHo, and he called me when he was nearby, in TriBeCa, where Manhattan falls off the grid and becomes a tangle of diagonal cross streets and dead ends.

"Tell me what corner you're at," I said, looking at a map online, "and I'll tell you how to get here."

"I don't know where I am!"

"Don't you see any street signs? Look up."

"Leigh. Just come and get me," he said.

I told my coworkers I'd be back in a few minutes, and went to go claim him, like a child who'd gotten lost at a theme park. We reunited beneath the marquee for the Tribeca Film Festival. Jason was wearing a large camping backpack over a tight gray shirt made out of some space-age sweat-proof fabric. He was sweating a lot. His hair was buzzed, and it made his face look big, mean.

"Hi," I said.

"Oh, hey." Neither of us touched. We'd talked on the phone

for hours, anticipating this moment, but nothing could have prepared us for what it was actually like to stand face-to-face again
for the first time in two years. My point of view had completely
changed. I'd wanted him to come visit so I could see him, but I
no longer had any desperate hopes for our future. I just wanted to
have a good time. If that sounds naïve, it's because it was—I
thought I was tough enough to spend a week with Jason and have
nothing but "good times." I thought he wouldn't be able to hurt
me anymore because now I was strong enough to stop him.

We walked back to my office so I could finish my workday.
"This is my friend Jason," I announced to my coworkers, which
seemed like the simplest way to describe him, even though it
wasn't true. We'd never been friends. In the back of the office,
under a skylight, there was a wicker couch with pastel floral
upholstery, and that's where he sat quietly, the rest of the afternoon, reading the news off his laptop. *So far so good*, I thought.
He hadn't said or done anything rude or strange that I would
later have to apologize for, in his absence.

At six o'clock, we took the subway to my place. After swear-
ing as a teenager that I would leave the suburbs as soon as I could,
I had settled down in a Brooklyn neighborhood that was practi-
cally pastoral. The streets, lined with old sycamores, were safe
enough for kids to bike alone, and on Saturdays I could smell
freshly mowed grass. Every morning I woke to birdsong. I shared
an apartment on the second floor of a Victorian house with three
other women. Our apartment was quirky and charming: we had
a terrace covered in AstroTurf, a bathroom door we could never
close completely because it was swollen in its frame in all weather,
and a trapezoidal living room with built-in shelving.

In my cozy room, my bed, desk, bookshelves, and keyboard took up almost all the square footage. When we got there, Jason sat cross-legged on the hardwood floor, unzipped his backpack, and removed a gallon-sized Ziploc bag filled with pills.

"What is all that?"

"Vitamins. Antioxidants. Fish oil, zinc, Adderall, Klonopin." By color, shape, and size, he could distinguish between the pills, and he swallowed them in strategic handfuls. "I'm doing an experiment on longevity."

"I know," I said. "You told me." I remembered his most recent e-mail: *Immortality ahoy?*

I couldn't tell if he looked healthy or not. He was built-up, huge, from working out; his triceps looked like wings trying to push through the skin of his arms. Watching him sort through the stuff he'd packed for his stay, I remembered how much I'd once loved being his audience. But this time, I was slightly on edge. Jason was twitchy. He could focus intently for a few minutes, and then his mind would be racing elsewhere. *ADD*, I thought to myself. *So ADD!* But according to the e-mail he'd sent me, his experiments made him feel *more focused and "smarter."*

"I got a bottle of wine and thought we could make pesto for dinner. Okay with you?"

He was staring at me.

"What?" I said.

"You're so confident now. It makes you sexy."

I rolled my eyes, secretly flattered on behalf of the insecure twenty-two-year-old inside me. He put the pills away, and we sat beside each other on my bed, on top of the same hot pink satin quilt that had covered our bed in Albuquerque. I had the standing fan in the corner by the window turned up to high. Jason seemed nervous, so I kissed him first. He kissed back, and pulled down the straps of my dress. "Your boobs have gotten bigger."

"Maybe."

We lay down. More clothes came off. Jason paused the kissing and held my face. "Leigh," he said. "I've thought a lot about how I treated you when we lived together, and I want to be so good to you now that it makes up for every horrible thing I did." I didn't know what to say. It sounded like a cliché line a bad boyfriend would give his woman to get her to forgive him, but it wasn't a cliché for Jason because he never said anything like it. The closest thing it reminded me of was a time in Albuquerque when he'd gotten into bed with me and cried, "I don't know what I'd do if something bad happened to you. I don't know what I'd do." Back then, I'd thought that true love meant making yourself sick imagining something horrible happening to your beloved, and predicting how you yourself would be destroyed without them.

"That's nice," I said, and unbuckled his belt.

"Wait," he said, stopping my hands. "We need a condom."

"I have condoms," I said.

"What kind? I only use female condoms now."

"What?"

"They're so much better. I met this woman in Little Rock who—"

"I don't want to hear about the woman in Little Rock. Can't you just use what I have?"

But no. He refused to use the condoms I had and I gave up on arguing, got dressed, and agreed to walk to the drugstore with him. Darnell, the cute checkout guy, was working. I avoided eye contact and took a circuitous route to the "family planning" section, skulking like a teenager. The drugstore didn't have any female condoms. I walked outside and waited for Jason, who finally came out, wearing a grin. "Darnell is gonna hook us up with some weed."

"Jesus Christ."

"What?"

"You've been in New York for like four hours and you're already trying to score weed?"

"Hey," Jason said, "I'm on vacation."

Back at my apartment, we started fooling around again. He didn't want to use the condoms I had and I said to just forget the condoms, I was on the pill. What could go wrong? He'd already given me HPV. But what if he gave me HIV? I'm sure the number of women he'd slept with was in the triple digits. I was being stupid; I *knew* I was being stupid, and yet I didn't care. We were repeating our entire relationship at hyperspeed: I was tired of being in my head. I wanted to be in my body; I wanted to take what I wanted from him. The golden light of early summer evening shot through the windows and I was naked and unselfconscious. We fucked for a long time. He remembered every way I liked to be touched, as if he'd written the book on my body. There was just no comparing the way Jason touched me to the way I'd been touched by anyone else.

In my memory, it's the best sex we ever had, but that's what memory does: lets you shape a raw experience into a story you can tell yourself later.

The next day, I worked from home. I told Jason he could go out and explore without me, but he said, "I just want to be with you, okay? I just want to do everything with you." He went to the liquor store when it opened and bought a jumbo bottle of white wine, which he began drinking around noon. While I was on the phone with my boss, he wrote me a note: *May I have an Ativan?* I looked away while he crushed the pills on my desk and snorted them up his nose.

In the afternoon I got high with him because I thought then this would all seem more fun. We stood by my open bedroom window, which overlooked a playhouse in the driveway for the toddler who lived upstairs. I was scared that my landlord (a mother of two) would smell the smoke and say something, but part of Jason's black magic was that he made me, a usually responsible adult, become completely irresponsible. He gave me permission to be a fuckup.

"Next time, you'll come visit me, and we'll go camping in the Ozarks," he said, sucking on the joint.

"No, I won't," I said. "I hate camping."

"You don't know how beautiful it is."

"You're right, I don't know how beautiful it is, *but I still don't like camping.*" I was coughing too much to fully inhale, so I closed my eyes and Jason blew the smoke right into my mouth.

"I think about moving back all the time," he said.

"To New Mexico?"

"Leigh, let's go back. And just live off the land."

All our old dreams now sounded like nightmares. Jason was living with his grandmother in Little Rock, working odd jobs, trying to go back to school. From the time I'd met him, when he was about to turn nineteen, until now, at the age twenty-three, Jason had always seemed on the verge of success, but never once actually successful. That verge used to unify us, when it was us against the world who didn't believe in our dreams, but now it just showed how different our lives were. I was happy in Brooklyn. I had a good job and good friends and the novel I'd written in Albuquerque had been picked up by a publisher. My life was no longer about planning my next escape.

The week before Jason came, Brian and I had our second first date, after we'd broken up and he'd dreamed of me in Italy. We met for a walk in Prospect Park, and stood still on a small bridge overlooking a beautiful wedding on the lake. Brian kissed the back of my neck and whispered that he was sorry for everything that had happened between us. We walked from one end of the park to the other, until we were closer to my neighborhood than his, and went to dinner at my favorite restaurant.

"So your back is better?"

"So much better. I could even dance if I wanted to. Not just slow-dance, but like Irish line dancing."

I had almost forgotten how funny Brian was. When I told him I was geeking out because I had my own ISBN now for my novel, he said, "Usually Jews don't like getting assigned a number, but in your case, that's awesome."

We were sitting outside on the restaurant's back patio, eating french fries. The evening was unusually cool, and Brian snuggled in closer toward me for warmth, an absurd gesture from someone a foot taller than I am. "Get out of here," I said. "I'm the lady; you're supposed to put your arm around *me* and ask if *I'm* cold."

He put his arm around me and pulled me closer. "What are you doing next week?"

I froze in his embrace. Did he somehow already know what I was doing? "Why do you ask?"

"I'm going to the Provincetown Film Festival for work and wanted to see if you'd like to come with me. On a road trip."

"Oh, I would love to, but . . ." I tried to think of how I wanted to put this. Part of me felt duplicitous that I was going from seeing one guy to seeing another, but another part of me felt defensive. What, I was just supposed to wait for Brian for months, assuming he would want to get back together with me? I wasn't supposed to make any plans? It was none of his business that Jason was coming to visit.

"I have a friend in town next week," I said.

"Who?"

"Just an old friend."

"You mean a guy friend."

"Yes," I said.

"He's staying with you?"

"Yes."

I waited for some kind of reaction, but Brian didn't say anything else. I had never told him enough about Jason for him to put the pieces together, for him to worry.

On the second day of Jason's visit, we went to this same restaurant. He was drunk and high. I was high and tired. I could not keep up with one-tenth of the amount of drugs and alcohol Jason was consuming that week, and no matter how much I drank or smoked,

I still wasn't having fun. He ordered a steak and two glasses of scotch, and I had a cheeseburger. We had nothing to talk about. Unless I was willing to participate in his fantasy of us moving back to the desert together, there was nothing to say.

After dinner, he wanted to go out and keep drinking, and I wanted to crash. I gave him my house keys and offered to tell him where the bars were.

"I'll find them," he said, and left.

By four thirty in the morning he still wasn't back. Between night and dawn, the sky poured rain. I tried texting and calling, but there was no answer. I felt more pissed off than worried, and lay in bed, unable to fall back asleep, listening to the rain and the occasional whoosh of a car on the street. When he finally burst through my bedroom door, Jason was dripping wet.

He peeled off his clothes and dropped them; his belt buckle made a thud against the hardwood floor. "I went to this bar on Coney Island Avenue and there was this group of gay guys all talking to me and buying me drinks and the bartender was giving me all my drinks for free."

"Why?" I asked, even though I already knew the answer to my own question: he'd found a rapt audience.

"Because they liked me! Then the bartender had to close, and it was raining, so I went home with her."

"You went home with the bartender," I repeated.

"It was raining!"

I didn't even want to know what he did after he went home with the bartender. I didn't ask. I went back to sleep. By eight in the morning, he was wide-awake, jumping on the bed, trying to wake me up, too, so we could start the day. "You're being boring," he told me, as I tried to bury my face deeper into my pillow. When I told the story of the bartender to Callista at the funeral, she said, "I can't believe he did that to you, Leigh," and I saw that she felt more pity for me than I'd felt for myself. I was so braced to be hurt by him by that point that nothing he did was beyond the realm of possibility.

The next four days in Brooklyn passed in a blur. I stayed as drunk or high as I possibly could, so I would be numb to what was happening. We got in a fight at the Coney Island Mermaid Parade because he was tired of walking and I was tired of him complaining. We got in a fight in Central Park in the rain over something that I've now totally forgotten. We had dinner with my friend Sarah and her boyfriend, and Jason avoided eye contact with both of them and blatantly ate a sandwich he'd pulled out of his backpack, before our entrées arrived. I canceled all the plans I'd made for him to meet my other friends. I gave him my house keys so he could go out at night while I slept alone. We did not have sex again.

Jason's visit was a trap I'd built myself and then walked right into. I couldn't wait for him to leave so I could go back to work, so I could see Brian again. The trap I'd built was also my own liberation: his visit had finally made me see that I no longer wanted this person to be a part of my life. The morning he left for the airport, I kissed him good-bye. Then I went to work and after work I went over to Brian's and I made a promise to myself that I would never answer Jason's phone calls or texts again.

For the first time, it felt like I had a choice. I didn't have to be the tragic heroine of my own life anymore. I didn't have to play Medea or Alcestis or a *rusalka* or La Llorona or Sylvia Plath, women spurned and vengeful and suicidal and martyred for love. Seeing Jason in the context of the life I'd rebuilt in New York gave me the clarity to cut his character from the script, and the power to put the ending on our story.

Within a month, he had stabbed a man in Little Rock. Eleven days after that, he was dead.

For so many years, I never felt like I could tell the truth about my relationship with Jason, because then there would be no sympathy for me. *He hit you? Then why didn't you leave him?* And then I couldn't reveal everything that happened the summer of his death, because then there would be no sympathy for him. *He died young, so what? He stabbed someone!*

I wanted sympathy for both of us. I thought maybe it was a matter of getting the facts straight. Maybe I was having trouble telling a sympathetic story because I didn't have all the information.

So I decided that if I could just get a copy of the police report, I would be able to put that summer back together. I thought I'd be able to draw a clear straight line between our visit, his crime, and the accident, and then the story of our lives together would finally make sense.

Three years after his death, I obtained the incident report from the night of the stabbing.

Suspect is light complexioned, with medium, straight, brown hair. The color of the suspect's eyes is unknown. The suspect is clean shaven. Exact Age: 23. Weight: 190. Is the suspect MENTALLY AFFLICTED? Unknown.

At 5:40 a.m. on July 10, 2011, a convenience store clerk called the police after a girl (a "female juvenile") entered the store and told him that her father had been stabbed. When the police officer arrived at the scene, Jason was sitting on the curb and told the officer, "I was getting on my motorcycle when a white male approached me and asked me for money. I told him I did not have any and he walked toward his car. I went to a nearby vehicle to bum a cigarette. The white male said, 'What did you say about me?' and came at me. We fought and I pulled my knife to defend myself. He went back to his vehicle and ran over me and my motorcycle and left the area."

There was a large amount of blood on the concrete, but Jason wasn't injured. The officer asked Jason who got cut. Jason said he didn't know. The officer repeated his question multiple times. Finally Jason said, "Someone might have gotten cut," and pulled the knife from his pocket. It was covered in blood.

The first few times I read this, I thought Jason sounded like he was out of his mind. And if he sounded out of his mind, it meant either the report was badly written and I could criticize and dismiss it, or it meant that he was actually having some kind of psychotic break and I could forgive him because he didn't know what he was saying or doing. Either way I was on his side. Then again, under the category of "demeanor," there's a check mark next to "calm." Jason knew how to talk to police, so maybe he wasn't out of his mind; maybe this was just sophisticated manipulation and I was falling for it yet again.

It finally dawned on me that Jason must have been manic that summer—from his Brooklyn visit to the stabbing to the deadly accident. I flashed back to the bipolar disorder medication I'd found in his bathroom when we first started dating. I replayed a mental montage of his visit: bag of pills, bottle of wine, jumping on the bed after three hours of sleep. I thought about his final e-mail, about his self-designed experiment on longevity, and his theory on using Adderall and bupropion cyclically, to treat depression:

> *When ceasing bupropion you have to gradually decrease the dosage due to the possibility of SNRI withdrawal symptoms- this is very common when dealing with ss and SNRIs. However, due to the mood-elevating properties strongly associated with amphetamine salts, you could most likely avoid the side effects that frequently include irritability, and recurrence of depressive symptoms. This could likely hold true for the opposite, decreasing Adderall and increasing bupropion, due to their similar effects regarding noradrenergic and dopaminergic activity.*

His e-mail didn't make sense to me when I read it the first, second, or third time. I thought I was just too ignorant to understand the science behind the drugs, but over time it became evidence of the flights of his manic mind.

Poor Jason, I thought. *A victim of mental illness.* No matter what he did to me during the four and half years we knew each other, I'd always found it much easier to award the role of victim to Jason than to consider that the role might be mine. Maybe that's because when he was alive, he'd accused me of always casting myself as the victim in my stories, and the only way to prove him wrong was to stop admitting that he was hurting me. I so rarely described Jason to anyone as "abusive," because I thought then I would be in the position of explaining why I didn't cut him out of my life—why, instead, I always yearned for him to stay in it.

But this was a report of a crime, and it scared me to think my brain was still calibrated to his specifications, that I could read a narrative of what he'd done and still frame him in my mind as the victim.

For so long, I struggled to come up with an explanation for why our lives seemed so inseparably intertwined, for why I went back to him so many times when his behavior should have kept me away. Was it his charisma? My insecurity, naïveté? Our youth? Was I seduced by the idea that there was this one person for me who, for better or worse, I would never escape?

I never found the answers, but now I don't think I need them.

I can reread the police report, all my diary entries, our e-mails, the poems I wrote him, every document I have of our lives together, but the stories I find there will always conflict, like dissonant piano chords. I can't bring them to resolve, no matter how many times I keep banging them out. I know that I love Jason, and I miss him—present tense. I also know that when I first heard about the stabbing, the thought flashed across my mind that I could have been the victim. Do I contradict myself? Now that Jason's gone, I finally have control of our story, and I'm leaving in the contradictions. Our story would be incomplete without them.

After his death, my mom planted a rosebush in Jason's honor, in the backyard garden that he helped to till for my parents when we first started dating.

"I wanted to choose one that made sense for Jason," she told me.

The rose she chose is called Knock Out.

How to Get Over It

(2011–14)

> *The young widow should wear deep crepe for*
> *a year and then lighter mourning for six months*
> *and second mourning for six months longer.*
> *There is nothing more utterly captivating than a*
> *sweet young face under a widow's veil, and it is*
> *not to be wondered at that her own loneliness*
> *and need of sympathy, combined with all that is*
> *appealing to sympathy in a man, results in the*
> *healing of her heart. She should, however, never*
> *remain in mourning for her first husband after*
> *she has decided she can be consoled by a second.*
>
> EMILY POST

Decide to get a tattoo.

Pick out a Georgia O'Keeffe watercolor of the sun burning as it sets because it reminds you of the bold daylight in New Mexico, and the moody blue nights when you could see all the stars. The sun on the horizon makes a red, horizontal *J*. You've never wanted a tattoo before, but you've also never had something you wanted your own body to always remind you of. *This is it*, you think. Loss is the story you want told across your shoulder.

"Don't get a tattoo right now," your mother says. "Not when you're so emotional." One of her rules to live by is *Don't make any big decisions when you're in a bad mood.* Another is: *Don't cry in front of a mirror; you'll only cry harder.* It's an empathic reaction. (Which is not to say that you have not occasionally, purposefully, violated these rules.)

"Why don't you just download the painting and put it as your computer background?" she asks.

Your boyfriend agrees with her, and there go your hopes for an ally in this. He says you should really think about it.

"But I have thought about it!"

"Jews aren't supposed to get tattoos anyway," he adds.

You go online and look it up. The Jewish prohibition against tattoos comes from Leviticus 19:28: "You shall not make gashes in your flesh for the dead, or incise any marks on yourselves: I am the Lord."

No one gets it: you *want* to gash your flesh for the dead. You want to be marked. And when strangers see what is on your skin, you'll be able to explain, *This is what I lost. This is what I have to live the rest of my life without.*

If anyone should understand your motivations, it's him, this man you've just moved in with, in the wake of your loss (see: *Don't make any big decisions when you're in a bad mood*). His grandfather has the indelible mark of a serial number on his arm from Auschwitz. He tells you that in high school he wanted to get the same number tattooed on his own arm—as a reminder of what could happen. What *did* happen. His mother was horrified. She forbade it.

Seeking a third opinion (seeking permission), over coffee

you ask your sophisticated friend Cathrin with the pretty, coppery eyeshadow if she's ever thought of getting a tattoo, and the answer is yes. She has it all thought out; it will be a German word (her mother tongue) on the inside of her right forearm.

"What word?"

"Longing."

"What is it in German?"

"*Sehnsucht.*" She writes it for you on a napkin. "This first part, *sehn*, is longing. But the second part, *sucht*, comes from addiction."

In essence, you both want the same tattoo, but yours is an image, and hers is a word. You could fill a catalog with all you long for—for him to come back, for a do over, for a different ending in which not only were you strong and said good-bye but he lived and made a success of his life and decades later you could look back together on your twenties and laugh at all your follies, for his voice on the other end of a phone call, for one more of those Albuquerque nights when it was easy to fall asleep knowing he was just in the next room.

After Cathrin gives her blessing for your tattoo, you realize you may have mistaken your own desire. Maybe you didn't want a tattoo. Maybe you just needed to talk to someone who understands this kind of longing.

Go to therapy.

You were planning to go anyway; you've actually been waiting six weeks to be seen at a low-cost clinic in Brooklyn. Your first appointment is a few days after his funeral.

"I've just been to a funeral," you tell the social worker. She is only a few years older than you, with long plain hair and eyes that listen to everything you say. Like yours, her mother is a therapist. Every Thursday night you sit in her small office and cry for forty-five minutes. The tears arrive like a Pavlovian response to her sympathy; you can't help but cry. On nights when there isn't much to talk about, you trade book recommendations, talk about feminism.

Your therapist won't use the word *abusive* until you do. It will take three years before you are able to say it, seriously, in her office, without using scare quotes.

Read all the books.

Read the books by the woman who lost her husband and then her daughter, the book by the man who lost his wife, the book by the woman who lost her mother, the book by the woman whose husband's helicopter crashed in Iraq. Read the book by the woman who became best friends with a woman on death row in Texas, after her own son died in an accident. Read the book about the sick kids who draw pictures of the afterlife because they know that's where they're going. Read the book by the woman who lost her baby. Read the book by the man who accidentally killed a girl when they were both teenagers. Read about the friend lost to suicide (a train), the mother lost to suicide (an overdose), the young wife lost to suicide (an overdose). Read the memoir disguised as a novel about the young wife taken by a wave.

None of these stories are your stories.

And yet all of these stories are your stories, if you extrapolate the data. The beloved husband becomes your boy; the mother lost to cancer becomes your boy; the prisoner whose time has run out becomes him, too.

There is an endless supply of these books. You could never read all of them in your lifetime. The shape and shadow of each loss is unique, but you can always recognize the grieving by their disbelief, their struggle to make sense of tragic senselessness, their desperation for a different ending to a story that has already reached its conclusion.

The cover of one of these books—*A Grief Observed* by C. S. Lewis—proclaims it is "a masterpiece of rediscovered faith which has comforted thousands." You regret ordering this particular paperback edition (used) off the Internet. You reject the word *comfort*, the idea that any of these texts could take some of your sorrow away from you. *Comfort* sounds like a fix, and you don't want to be fixed. Mostly what you like about all these books is getting to sit with their authors, their confused and angry and unwashed selves, overhearing their ambivalent thoughts. You like it when you get to the end of the book and they still don't have any good answers to the questions of *why* and *how* that haunt them. So often these books end with a beautiful memory, a dream, a good-bye, or a wish. But you want to know what happens to him or her, the narrator, the survivor, who still has to go on living after the last page.

Become a woman who can form an instant friendship with anyone who has lost a parent, child, friend, or lover. It's a club. You're a member. Though he rarely talks about it, your boyfriend also belongs; he lost his dad to cancer when he was twenty-seven. When you watch old movies together, he likes to guess which actors are gone and which, unbelievably, are still alive.

How quickly the membership grows. You memorize the line, *Lovely to meet you. So sorry it was under these circumstances.*

In Dodge City, Kansas, you attend the funeral of your thirty-two-year-old cousin, found dead in a basement apartment near a meatpacking plant. A few months later there's a funeral in a cathedral on the Jersey Shore for a girl whose suicide no one is naming a suicide; her mother's black flip-flops slap the cold marble floor. Your best friend loses both her parents in quick succession, calls you when you're eating a sandwich in Miami Beach to tell you how her dad was found, and you go to Philadelphia to hear her deliver a eulogy and help transport an elderly cat. You do your best saying kaddish for your boyfriend's grandfather who survived the camps, and go to Long Island on your twenty-ninth birthday for the headstone unveiling. After the service, someone hands you a big piece of cake.

"We don't have weddings in our family," your boyfriend's great-aunt explains. "We have funerals."

Get married.

Isn't that what's supposed to happen next?

You've been waiting for the end of this chapter of your life to present itself, like the finish line of a marathon, and maybe this is what you've been waiting for. Marriage seems like the happy ending your family wants for you. So why do you resist?

It's not that you don't love him, this tall, kind, private person whom you've lived with for one, two, three years, more. Soon you will have known him for even longer than you knew the boy who died. But a wedding wouldn't change what you have or what you lost or who you are. Your *getting over it* does not mean an aisle where one him is replaced by another.

Signs

(2014)

Where I was born and where and how I have
lived is unimportant. It is what I have done with
where I have been that should be of interest.

GEORGIA O'KEEFFE

Before I went back, I told everyone where I was going. And in response, they all said, *You're going to Mexico? By yourself?* One friend sent an e-mail to say, *Have a great time in Arizona.*

It felt as if I was returning to a state that existed only in my mind. A mental state known as the Land of Enchantment. For almost three years I imagined what it would be like to go back there without Jason in the driver's seat, without any way to reach him and say, *Remember this?* and it was trepidation that prevented me from making a move. I was afraid of how badly I wanted this return trip to mean something. But what if my expectations were dangerously high? What if I got all the way out there, stood under the banner of that sky, and felt nothing? What if that land was, just as my relationship with Jason had been, more beautiful in memory than in life?

When I get there, I thought, *the sign that I'm where I'm supposed to be will be waiting for me.* Even though I envied the signs

Callista seemed to always be receiving from the beyond, I already had so many signs I could remember interpreting when Jason was still alive: signs that we should be together, signs that we should stay apart, signs that staying apart would never work and that in the end I would always be tied to him, for better or worse. And then there were the signs that he would die young, never see thirty, and he knew it.

Jason's childhood sweetheart wasn't at his funeral. I'd never met her, but I'd spent plenty of time jealously and obsessively imagining their relationship: how they rode the school bus together, how they rode the Ferris wheel at Navy Pier when she came to visit. She was his first love and she always would be, which might be okay, I used to think, as long as I could be his last. I blamed her for ruining my twenty-third birthday in Albuquerque by mailing Jason a romantic photo scrapbook (I was the one who checked the mail). He locked it in the briefcase he'd bought at Salvation Army, but I found the key and looked at it while he was at work. The birthday was ruined when I told him I'd seen everything, including pictures of her in brown lingerie.

"That wasn't lingerie," he argued, "that was her nightgown."

At the funeral, I asked if anyone had called Becca to tell her.

"She's nine months pregnant," his brother told me. "We called her family but they didn't want to . . . to jeopardize the pregnancy."

Six months later, she sent me a message on Facebook:

You don't know me. It took ten years, but Jason managed to make me fall for him, too. I'll never forget what he told me one day (during the days he thought he was James Dean).

Jason: "I won't live to be twenty-seven."

Me: "Don't say that! Yes, you will."

(And then every day of my life after we stopped talking-
he will live right? he's still okay today, right?)

Gah, I wish I had called him one last time. I had long
since married and moved on from Jason's violent and crazy
life, but he always hid deep in a tiny spot of my heart.

You don't know me. I kept returning to this line. I knew
enough. I wish I could say we were in some kind of sorority of
exes together, Phi Beta Eros, but Becca had "moved on," the way
characters do in books—marry another man, have a baby. Without a husband or a child to hold, I was stuck cherishing what I'd
lost instead of what I'd found. But maybe there was another
ending waiting for me? Another kind of "getting over"?

As time passed, I did the most ordinary thing: I got older. I
loosened my grip on this hurt, and my petty grievances toward
Becca. When I finally went back to New Mexico, three years
after Jason's death, I wasn't looking for signs that I was most
beloved, treasured even from beyond. Still, I thought I would
feel Jason with me, in the land that we called our own.

On the flight to Albuquerque, the baby in the row behind me
screamed for three hours while I tried to read a book with the
word *empathy* in the title. One of the book's chapters was called
"Pain Tours." Was I embarking upon one of those? I made conversation with the man seated beside me, who also lived in Brooklyn. His laptop was open to a spreadsheet that had something to

do with his health work in Africa that I didn't totally understand. He was on his way toward northern New Mexico, to spend spring break with his wife and children. They were seated a few rows ahead with his mother-in-law, who had long gray hair and silver and turquoise jewelry on all her exposed tan skin. She looked like so many other women I'd seen in Santa Fe or Albuquerque or Abiquiu—sun-stricken and stoic, O'Keeffe reincarnate, a vision of the aesthetic I fantasized for myself in forty or fifty years.

"And how about you? Work? Vacation?"

"I used to live in Albuquerque," I said, "with my boyfriend. And then he died. I'm going back for the first time."

"I'm sorry," he said.

"It's okay." I hadn't made him uncomfortable: that was good. *But this guy works with sick people in Africa*, I reminded myself, *he can handle it*. I remembered the tattoo I had wanted after Jason died, the watercolor painting that I thought could be my shorthand, my beautiful transition into the same sad story I found myself telling over and over again. I hated making other people uncomfortable, but I also felt a compulsion to say those words *and then he died* to everyone, lest they not understand where I was coming from.

When I lived in New York the first time, at nineteen, I worked every weekend at a nightclub checking coats until four in the morning, in a basement hallway that should have been a fire escape. One night I got carbon monoxide poisoning and blacked out (at least I think it was carbon monoxide poisoning: I didn't go to the hospital until the next day and they said it was most likely that, but too many hours had passed to officially test my blood). Then someone opened the door to the back alley and the smell of garbage and fish and night air came in, and I woke back up, had to keep working until we closed. I was going through a phase when I only wore the color pink, and my boss called me "sweet." In his West African accent he said, "Sweet, it's okay to feel a little pain and push through it because that's how you grow up." And I thought, *You don't know anything about me or my pain.* At that point, I had been medicated for depression for six years. I didn't know how to tell him he was wrong about me. I also didn't know that he was right: that there was still so much more pain to come, so much more growing up still left to do.

I'd always defined my adolescence by the depression and suicidal thoughts that shaped it. When I met Jason at twenty-two, the stories he told me of his own adolescence made mine seem so pale and ordinary in comparison. My twenties were ignited by his presence, and then clouded by the smoke of his absence. Although I could think of examples of how I'd "pushed through," the narrative I told about my life usually went, "And then this happened to me." I was ready for a future that was shaped not by what happened to me but rather by what I made happen.

In the airplane bathroom mirror, I found a new gray hair on my head and pulled it out. I was twenty-nine years old, a decade away from the girl who had passed out in the fire escape. If Jason was with me, he would have just had his twenty-sixth birthday. Unlike my lifeline, which felt like it extended toward the horizon indefinitely, Jason's was fixed in time, a finite number set: April 5, 1988–July 21, 2011. With those set dates, I could build a calendar of anniversaries: birthday, death day, day we met, day we moved, day we moved back, last morning I saw him. I could still remember the soft texture of his hair, even though he'd so rarely let me run my fingers through it. I thought I could remember what the sun felt like in New Mexico, and I was going back to see if my memory was accurate. Maybe that's what I use anniversaries for: to prick my memories, prove that I haven't forgotten a single thing.

The plane landed at the Albuquerque Sunport. I said goodbye to the man and went to claim my suitcase from the baggage carousel. I picked up my rental car and rolled down the windows. The sun I loved was setting, and the lights of the city sparkled against the russet horizon. I drove north.

I stayed in Albuquerque for a few days, eating green chile breakfast burritos and catching up with old friends. I went for a run in the Bosque, along a path framed by cottonwoods. I drove down Route 66, expecting to see something that I had forgotten was there, but the most surprising thing was that everything I saw— bus stop near the fairgrounds, faded sign above the taxidermy shop, Del Taco by the train tracks—matched the blueprint of my memory. I'd been haunting myself with visions of this place, but it wasn't gone or destroyed; the Land of Enchantment lived on.

And yet I found no sign of Jason anywhere.

None of the songs he loved played on the radio, I didn't find his name written on any dollar bills, no sunset evoked his spirit, and I wasn't visited in dreams. Had I really expected all that? Was that what I really wanted? I could try and convince myself that the absence of signs was, in itself, a sign: that Jason was finally leaving me alone, giving me his blessing to go on, but then I would have to admit that even from beyond he still had a say in my destiny.

I didn't want to give him that power anymore.

Every day I drove around the city that I loved, but I did not go back to our old apartment, to see the door on which Vicky knocked, the hot tub where José told us about La Llorona, the parking lot where Diane taught me how to drive her truck. I did not go back to the diner and ask one of the busboys to make me a coffee malt. I did not go back to Walmart to see if the coin-operated rides were still outside the front doors.

Look at me, here without him. Not for the first time, but for the first time without Jason at most a phone call away. And Brian was back in Brooklyn, because this was my journey to go on, not his. So where did that leave me, without a man to show me what kind of woman I was?

Before Jason's death, I was just starting to figure out the answer to that question—evidenced by the instinct I had to stop dating Brian when it wasn't working for me, the confidence Jason recognized in me during his last visit, and the courage I had to finally ignore his phone calls, after months and years of wishing I could.

It wasn't as easy as swapping out the bad guy for a good one. It was me. I was the one who had evolved, from the girl auditioning for every girlfriend role, trying to be so cool and nice and interesting and funny but also as beautiful as possible and sexy and never a nag or a victim or a drag, to the woman who could quit acting and just say, *This is it. This is who I am.*

Though we'd lived in New Mexico for only six months, Jason and I had spent years in a state of enchantment. In our isolated and sometimes beautiful kingdom, each moment was so intense and vivid, I felt spellbound to stay. Even when I recognized the cycle of abuse, I was convinced that if I left the lows behind I would never again have another high. The fact that my friends and family had such a hard time understanding this seemed like yet another sign that Jason and I belonged in a kingdom apart.

When Jason worked as a security guard for the movie studios in Albuquerque, he had a lot of time to sit around, so I checked out books for him from the library, or he read whatever I'd checked out for myself. For a week we shared a single copy of *Chilly Scenes of Winter* by Ann Beattie, trading it back and forth every fifty or a hundred pages.

Toward the end of that week, Jason shook me awake in bed. "Do you think Charles is going to get her back?"

"Get who back?" I mumbled.

"Laura! In the book!"

I laughed when I realized he'd rather ask me, since I had finished the novel first, than flip ahead and find out for himself. "Not telling," I said, and went back to sleep.

In this way, I used to want to know the ending to our own story. I collected signs as a way to flip ahead and predict the future.

Maybe I wasn't supposed to return to New Mexico to look for signs.

Maybe I was supposed to return to see how I could live without them.

Epilogue
(2015)

A few days before I finished writing this book, my bedroom at my parents' house in Illinois caught fire from a candle placed too close to some window curtains. My mom and dad ran outside in their pajamas, but their beloved cat was lost inside the black smoke and did not come when called. The firefighters carried his small body out of the house shrouded in a towel.

When I got the phone call about what had happened, all I could think about was that cat, terrified and confused, spending the last moments of his life unable to hear or see a way out.

It was a day or two later before I began to mentally inventory what was also lost: the notebooks in which I'd copied Plath poems at thirteen, the shoe box containing Daniel's letter to me on *Beauty and the Beast* stationery, my singing trophies, all my play scripts, the toy alligator souvenir, the books and bookshelves Jason once threatened to burn if I didn't go back to him in Albuquerque.

On the wall of my bedroom, there was a four-foot-high panel

of wallpaper depicting Gustav Klimt's ornate gold painting of Adele Bloch—red lips slightly parted, her long neck braced with pearls. When this, too, burned, the fire left another image behind in its place. "Like *The Twilight Zone*," my mom told me over the phone.

"What do you mean?"

She texted me a photo. There was another face now. Not where Adele's had been—high, nearing the ceiling—but in the lower left-hand corner, at the boundary where the painting ended and the wall began.

I knew right away whose face it was.

It was my face. The plain dark hair, the bold brow and dark lashes, flat planes of my cheeks.

"It kind of looks like my face?" I texted back, implying doubt even though I felt certain, in case she didn't see the same thing that I did.

"To me it looks more like Botticelli's Venus. But yes, clearly a face! So weird, right?"

I looked again. I didn't see Venus. *No*, I wanted to say, *you're wrong*. But maybe we each saw what we wanted to see. It was an optical illusion that symbolized how differently we viewed *moving on*. It was my mom who'd lit the candle that had set the curtains aflame, but she could overcome this tragic accident if she visualized the face of a goddess reborn from the ashes. I wanted to see a part of myself left behind in that room, so I could mourn her.

I know I'm a dweller. I ruminate; I replay memories. I knew Jason for four and a half years, and spent the next four unraveling our relationship and examining how it shaped the woman I've become. My mother is the opposite of a dweller. She is a healer, a fixer, a silver-lining seeker. When I was suicidal, a doctor's appointment was made, medication prescribed. When Jason broke my heart, she ordered a self-help book. When we moved to New Mexico, more self-help books. Albuquerque became our family's vacation destination once my complicated relationship was removed from the equation.

To a healer or a fixer, my dwelling might seem depressive and counterproductive, like I'm stalling the forward momentum of my destiny. But I'm at peace with the darkness in life coexisting with the bright spots. I can grip a fistful of losses in one hand, and still carry a handful of beautiful moments in the other.

In the summer of 2014, a few months after I went back by myself to New Mexico, Brian and I took a vacation to Prague and Budapest. There are photos of us standing on the Charles Bridge, sitting in a booth at the opera, riding the funicular down from Buda Castle. Brian's arms are so long that our selfies look like they were taken by a stranger on the street.

I had my laptop with me on vacation, and whenever we weren't sightseeing I was obsessively checking updates in a secret Facebook group for women writers. The group was only a few months old, but it had grown from a few dozen members to tens of thousands of members, almost overnight. I saw women posting that they'd never had the guts to submit to their dream publications before. I saw other women cheering them on, sharing connections, and stories of sexism and racism faced in their fields. I felt like a teenager again, forming intimate alliances with women I'd never met, typing little messages of courage and hope and sympathy at all hours of the day and night.

When Brian and I got back to New York, I slept and slept and slept and when I woke up, I had an idea.

Maybe we should all get together and have a conference, I typed to the group.

After a dozen immediate "likes" on my post, I stood up from my desk. "I've decided to organize a conference," I announced to Brian.

He took a deep breath. "A conference is a lot of work," he said gently.

"I know that!" I snapped. Of course I didn't know. I had no idea how much work it would be, no vision of the twelve-hour days ahead, but Brian's subtle skepticism of my plan made me doubly determined to accomplish it.

Within hours I found a cochair, and we started brainstorming how we would raise all the money we needed to bring hundreds of women together in New York.

"I need to buy a domain name for us," I said to Brian. We were calling our organization Out of the Binders, after the Mitt Romney gaffe about having binders full of women, but outofthebinders.com seemed long and unmemorable.

"Why don't you just call it BinderCon," he suggested.

Over the next three months, with the help of a couple dozen volunteers, my cochair and I sold tickets and awarded scholarships to BinderCon. We rented five venues over the course of two days, booked eighty speakers, and ordered hundreds of hot pink tote bags.

In October, my mom and sister came from Chicago. A couple of the women I'd met on LiveJournal ten years before flew in from California. There were more than five hundred women there—including my friend Julia.

On the first morning of the conference, standing at the podium in Cooper Union's Great Hall, I delivered a short speech. I told the story of the ugly winter after our lease was up in Albuquerque, when I was living back at my parents' house for the fourth time, missing Jason and hating myself for missing him, temping at the sump pump company where I was not allowed to read, and then I got Julia's e-mail that said she might have a job for me in New York.

"It's hard to imagine what my life would be like today," I said, "if Julia hadn't convinced me to send my résumé, and if I hadn't taken the leap, as much as I was terrified to leap, terrified to even lift one toe."

I knew so intimately what it was to be afraid. I was afraid of leaving Jason; I was afraid of staying with Jason; I was afraid of telling anyone the truth about our relationship for fear they would make the decision for me. I was afraid that I would be dependent, living with my parents forever, and I was also afraid that the job prospect was too good to be true.

But when I spoke in front of all those women, for the first time I felt that I could translate my personal experience into a story that would help someone else. "We all need Julias in our lives, friends who push us to be our most excellent selves," I continued, "but we also have to do the hard work of pushing past our own fears and doubts.

"And so today I dare you to do the thing you don't think you're ready to do."

It was the message I had once needed to hear. It just took years to find it.

ACKNOWLEDGMENTS

For believing in me and this book, I wish to thank Julia Phillips, Ellen Dworsky, Liz Hildreth, Alizah Salario, Claire Dunnington, Cathrin Wirtz, Nathan Ihara, and Jennie Baird. I am very grateful to Erin Hosier for adopting me and always responding to my e-mails within twenty-four hours, and to everyone at Plume, especially Kate Napolitano, for her wisdom and guidance, but also David Rosenthal, Joanna Kamouh, Jason Booher, and Andrea Santoro. Thank you to Matthew Daddona, Sarah Bridgins, and Rachel Bressler for their early support, and to Doree Shafrir at *BuzzFeed*, Kiese Laymon at *Gawker*, and Rebecca Soffer at *Modern Loss*, for publishing essays related to this book. I am grateful for the insights of my teachers Zia Jaffrey, Karen Karbo, and Beverly Lowry. Mom and Dad and Hattie, thank you for understanding why I needed to write this; I love you. Binders, I love you, too. Brian says he is waiting for the movie version to find out what happens, but I hope he flips ahead to find this page where I say thank you for being my partner and giving me a room of my own.

WORKS CONSULTED

Books

Lisa Appignanesi, *Mad, Bad and Sad: A History of Women and the Mind Doctors* (New York: Norton, 2009).

Jeffrey Eugenides, *The Virgin Suicides* (New York: Picador, 1993).

Euripides, *Alcestis* in *Euripides I*, translated by Richmond Lattimore (Chicago: University of Chicago Press, 1955).

Euripedes, *The Medea* in *Euripides I*, translated by Rex Warner (Chicago: University of Chicago Press, 1955).

Angela Lambert, *The Lost Life of Eva Braun* (New York: St. Martin's Press, 2014).

Cathy Luchetti and Carol Olwell, eds., *Women of the West* (New York: Norton, 2001).

Roxana Robinson, *Georgia O'Keeffe* (Hanover and New London, New Hampshire: University Press of New England, 1989).

Elizabeth Winder, *Pain, Parties, Work: Sylvia Plath in New York, Summer 1953* (New York: HarperCollins, 2013).

Essays and Articles

Edwin G. Dexter, "Suicide and the Weather," *Popular Science Monthly* 58 (April 1901): 604–15.

Joan Didion, "Georgia O'Keeffe," *The White Album* (New York: Farrar, Straus and Giroux, 1990).

James C. Kaufman, "The Sylvia Plath Effect: Mental Illness in Eminent Creative Writers," *The Journal of Creative Behavior* 35, no. 1 (March 2001): 37–50.

John Moore, "'The Hieroglyphics of Love': The Torch Singers and Interpretation," *Popular Music* 8, no. 1 (January 1989): 31–58.

Eleni Petridou, Fotios C. Papadopoulos, Constantine E. Frangakis, Alkistis Shalkidou, and Dimitrios Trichopoulos, "A Role of Sunshine in the Triggering of Suicide," *Epidemiology* 13, no. 1 (January 2002): 106–9.

RESOURCES

When I started writing this book, it was because I thought that what happened to me had never happened to anyone else. By the time I finished, I understood I was writing the story of so many. Intimate-partner violence is a public health concern, and according to the most recent survey published by the CDC[1], more than one in three women and one in four men have experienced rape, physical violence, and/or stalking by an intimate partner in their lifetime. They also found that nearly half of all women and men (48.4 percent and 48.8 percent, respectively) have experienced "psychological aggression" by an intimate partner. Young people are most at risk: first occurrences of rape, violence, and/or stalking mostly occur before age twenty-five.

If you or someone you know is experiencing intimate-partner violence, resources and support are available to help you. Here are some:

The National Domestic Violence Hotline (NDVH) operates 24/7 in more than 170 languages, with a TTY line available for the deaf. 1-800-799-SAFE (7233), 1-800-787-3224 (TTY)

---

1 Black, M. C., Basile, K. C., Breiding, M. J., Smith, S. G., Walters, M. L., Merrick, M. T., Chen, J., and Stevens, M.R. (2011). *The National Intimate Partner and Sexual Violence Survey (NISVS)*: 2010 Summary Report. Atlanta, GA: National Center for Injury Prevention and Control, Centers for Disease Control and Prevention.

Crisis Text Line (http://www.crisistextline.org/)

Shalom Bayit (http://www.shalom-bayit.org/) is based in the Bay Area and seeks to end domestic violence in Jewish homes. Call (866) SHALOM-7 for help. Love Shouldn't Hurt (http://love-shouldnt -hurt.org/) is their youth program.

Metropolitan Family Services (https://www.metrofamily.org/) provides clinical services for survivors of partner abuse and their children, and for teens and children who have witnessed domestic violence. (Illinois)

Mujeres Latinas en Acción (http://www.mujereslatinasenaccion.org/) provides a twenty-four-hour crisis hotline, counseling, and court advocates. (Illinois)

The New Mexico Coalition Against Domestic Violence (http://www .nmcadv.org/) provides a list of statewide victim-services providers.

Day One (http://www.dayoneny.org/) partners with youth to end dating abuse and domestic violence through education, support services, and legal advocacy. (New York)

The New York City Anti-Violence Project (www.avp.org) empowers lesbian, gay, bisexual, transgender, queer, and HIV-affected communities and allies to end all forms of violence, and supports survivors through counseling and advocacy.

Safe Horizon (http://www.safehorizon.org/) provides free telephone hotlines 24/7 for victims of domestic violence, sexual assault, and homeless youth and teens. There is a special hotline for hearing-impaired clients, and the website (and hotline) is also available in Spanish. (New York)